BEYOND DEATH

BEYOND
DEATH

BEYOND DEATH

Visions of the Other Side

By Edgar Cayce

A.R.E. Press • Virginia Beach • Virginia

A.R.E. Press
215 67th Street
Virginia Beach, VA 23451-2061

Cayce, Edgar, 1877-1945.
  Beyond death : visions of the other side / by Edgar Cayce
    p.   cm.
  ISBN-13: 978-0-87604-529-9 (trade pbk.)
  1. Death. 2. Future life. I. Title.
  BF1311.F8C38 2007
  133.901'3—dc22

                                    2007045806

Editor's Note
All of Edgar Cayce's discourses are now available on CD-ROM from A.R.E. Press at arebookstore.com or 800-333-4499.

Cover design by Richard Boyle

Contents

Contents

Foreword
Who Was Edgar Cayce?

"It is a time in the earth when people everywhere seek to know more of the mysteries of the mind, the soul," said my grandfather, Edgar Cayce, from an unconscious trance from which he demonstrated a remarkable gift for clairvoyance.

His words are prophetic even today, as more and more Americans in these unsettled times are turning to psychic explanations for daily events. For example, according to a survey by the National Opinion Research Council nearly half of American adults believe they have been in contact with someone who has died, a figure twice that of ten years earlier. Two-thirds of all adults say they have had an ESP experience; ten years before that figure was only one-half.

Every culture throughout history has made note of its own members' gifted powers beyond the five senses. These rare individuals held special interest because they seemed able to provide solutions to life's pressing problems. America in the twenty-first century is no exception.

Edgar Cayce was perhaps the most famous and most carefully documented psychic of our time. He began to use his unusual abilities when he was a young man, and from then on for over forty years he would, usually twice a day, lie on a couch, go into a sleeplike state, and respond to questions. Over fourteen thousand of these discourses, called readings, were carefully transcribed by his secretary and preserved by the Edgar Cayce Foundation in Virginia Beach, Virginia. These psychic readings continue to provide inspiration, insight, and help with healing to tens of thousands of people.

Having only an eighth-grade education, Edgar Cayce lived a plain and simple life by the world's standards. As early as his childhood in Hopkinsville, Kentucky, however, he sensed that he had psychic ability. While alone one day he had a vision of a woman who told him he would have unusual power to help people. He also related experiences of "seeing" dead relatives. Once, while struggling with school lessons, he slept on his spelling book and awakened knowing the entire contents of the book.

As a young man he experimented with hypnosis to treat a recurring throat problem that caused him to lose his speech. He discovered that under hypnosis he could diagnose and describe treatments for the physical ailments of others, often without knowing or seeing the person with the ailment. People began to ask him other sorts of questions, and he found himself able to answer these as well.

In 1910 the *New York Times* published a two-page story with pictures about Edgar Cayce's psychic ability as described by a young physician, Wesley Ketchum, to a clinical research society in Boston. From that time on people from all over the country with every conceivable question sought his help.

In addition to his unusual talents, Cayce was a deeply religious man who taught Sunday school all of his adult life and read the entire Bible once for every year that he lived. He always tried to attune himself to God's will by studying the Scriptures and maintaining a rich prayer life, as well as by trying to be of service to those who came seeking help. He used his talents only for helpful purposes. Cayce's simplicity and humility and his commitment to doing good in the world continue to attract people to the story of his life and work and to the far-reaching information he gave.

Charles Thomas Cayce, Ph.D.
President
Edgar Cayce Foundation

Editor's Explanation of Cayce's Discourses

Edgar Cayce dictated all of his discourses from a self-induced trance. A stenographer took his discourses down in shorthand and later typed them. Copies were sent to the person or persons who had requested the psychic reading, and one was put into the files of the organization, which built up around Cayce over the years, the Association for Research and Enlightenment (better known as the A.R.E.).

In his normal consciousness, Edgar Cayce spoke with a Southern accent but in the same manner as any other American. However, from the trance state, he spoke in the manner of the King James Bible, using "thees" and "thous." In trance, his syntax was also unusual. He put phrases, clauses, and sentences together in a manner that slows down any reader and requires careful attention in order to be sure of his meaning. This caused his stenographer to adopt some unusual punctuation in order to put into sentence form some of the long, complex thoughts conveyed by Cayce while in trance. Also, many of his discourses are so jam-packed with information and insights that it requires that one slow down and read more carefully in order to fully understand what he is intending.

From his trance state, Cayce explained that he got his information from two sources: (1) the inquiring individual's mind, mostly from his or her deeper, subconscious mind and (2) from the Universal Consciousness, the infinite mind within which the entire universe is conscious. He explained that every action and thought of every individual makes an impression upon the Universal Consciousness, an impression that can be psychically read. He correlated this with the Hindu concept of an Akashic Record, which is an ethereal, fourth-dimensional film upon which actions and thoughts are recorded and can be read at any time.

When giving one of his famous health readings, called physical readings, Cayce acted as if he were actually scanning the entire body of the person, from the inside out! He explained that the subconscious mind of everyone contains all of the data on the condition of the physical body it inhabits, and Cayce simply connected with the patient's deeper mind. He could also give the cause of the condition, even if it was from early childhood or from many lifetimes ago in a previous incarnation of the soul. This was knowable because the soul remembers all of its experiences. He explained that deeper portions of the subconscious mind are the mind of the soul, and portions of the subconscious and the soul are in the body with the personality.

In life readings and topic readings, Cayce also connected with the subconscious minds of those inquiring as well as the Universal Consciousness.

Occasionally, Cayce would not have the material being requested, and he would say, "We do not have that here." This implied that Cayce's mind was more directed than one might think. He was not open to everything. From trance, he explained that the suggestion given at the beginning of one of his psychic readings so directed his deeper mind and focused it on the task or subject requested that he truly did not have other topics available. However, on a few occasions, he seemed able to shift topics in the middle of a reading.

The typed readings have a standard format. Numbers were used in the place of the name of the person or persons receiving the reading, and a dash system kept track of how many readings the person had received. For example, reading 137-5 was the fifth reading for Mr. [137]. At the top of the reading are the reading number, the date and location, and the names or numbers (for privacy) of those in attendance. Occasionally the stenographer would include a note about other conditions, such as the presence of a manuscript that the in-trance Cayce was supposed to view psychically and comment on. In many cases, I left in the entire format of a recorded reading, but sometimes only a paragraph or two were pertinent to our study, and then I only give the reading number.

As I explained, Cayce dictated all of these discourses while he was in trance. In most cases, he spoke in a monotone voice. However, he would sometimes elevate his volume when saying a word or phrase. In these instances, his stenographer usually typed these words with all-capital letters, to give the reader some sense of Cayce's increased volume. These all-capital letters have been changed to italic typeface for readability, as well as emphasis. In many cases, these words appear to be rightly accentuated in Cayce's discourses. However, in some cases, it is not clear why he raised his voice.

Another style that the stenographer adopted was to capitalize all of the letters in Cayce's many affirmations (positive-thought or prayer-like passages to be used by the recipient as a tool for focusing and/or raising consciousness). I have also changed these to upper- and lower-case letters and italicized them. Questions asked Cayce have also been italicized for easier reference.

Whenever his stenographer was not sure if she had written down the correct word or thought that she might have missed or misunderstood a word, she inserted suggested words, comments, and explanations in [brackets]. If she knew of another reading that had similar material or that was being referred to during this reading, she would put the reading number in brackets. Cayce's entire collection of readings is available on CD-ROM from the A.R.E., so, even though the referenced reading may not be in this book, I left these references in for any future research; but several of the readings that have references are in this book. Within the text of a reading, all (parentheses) are asides made by Cayce himself while in trance, not by his stenographer. She only used [brackets] within the text of a reading. In the preliminary material, she used parentheses in the normal manner. My comments are indicated by the term "Editor's Note."

A few common abbreviations use in these discourses were: "GD" for Gladys Davis, the primary stenographer; "GC" for Gertrude Cayce, Edgar's wife and the predominant conductor of the readings; "EC" for Edgar Cayce; and "HLC" for Hugh Lynn Cayce, their son..

—John Van Auken, Editor

1

●

There Is No Death

Reading 5155-1

There is no death.

Reading 262-85

The *soul* cannot die; for it is of God. The body may be revivified, rejuvenated. And it is to that end it may, the body, *transcend* the earth and its influence.

Editor's Note: Edgar Cayce actually gives examples of ancient people who lived as long as they wanted—"dying" only when they chose to leave this world:

Reading 3579-1

The entity then lived to be a thousand years old, in years as termed today, and saw great changes come about.

Reading 823-1

For some six thousand years—if counted as time now—the entity journeyed with those people for the Yucatan land, or the establishing of the temple there in which the entity aided. But with those inroads from the children of Om and the peoples from the Lemurian land, or Mu, the entity withdrew into itself; taking—as it were—its own flight into the lands of Jupiter." This priestess lived six thousand years and died on her own terms, withdrawing from this world to sojourn in the non-physical dimensions of Jupiter.

Editor's note: Much more on this in the chapter on life beyond death.

Reading 1158-9

There is no life without death, there is no *renewal* without the dying of the old. Dying is not blotting out, it is transition. For it has ever been and is, even in materiality, a reciprocal world. "If ye will be my people, I will be thy God." If ye would know *good*, do good. If ye would have life, give life. If ye would know Jesus, the Christ, then be like Him; who died for a cause, without shame, without fault yet dying; and through that able to make what this season represents—*resurrection*!

Resurrection means what? It is reciprocal of that which has been expressed. How hath it been put again by him whom ye knew but disliked (for ye loved Peter the better)? "There is no life without death, there is no *renewal* without the dying of the old." Dying is not blotting out, it is transition—and ye may know transition by that as comes into the experience by those very activities, that "With what measure ye mete it shall be measured to thee again." That was His life, that is thy life, that is each one's life. Then how near, how dear has grown in the hearts, in the minds of all, those who put away self that they may know Him the better?

He put away self, letting it be nailed to the Cross; that the *new*, the renewing, the fulfilling, the *being* the Law, becomes the Law!

For it is the Law to *be* the Law, and the *Law* is Love!

Reading 5155-1

There is no death. Death is only overcome by Him, who has overcome death. It is our promise, and when ye abide in Him sufficient to that, ye with Him, as the resurrection, may indeed overcome death in a material sense.

Reading 136-18

Death is as but the beginning of another form of phenomenized force in the earth's plane, and may not be understood by the third dimension mind from third dimension analysis, but must be seen from that fourth-dimension force as may be experienced by an entity gaining the access to same, by development in the physical plane through the mental processes of an entity. The mind is being correlated with subconscious and spiritual forces that magnify same to the conscious force of an entity in such a manner as said entity gains the insight and concept of such phenomenized conditions, see?

We see in the physical world the condition in every form of life. As is taken here: We find in a grain of corn or wheat that germ that, set in motion through its natural process with Mother Earth and the elements about same, brings forth corn *after its kind*, see? the kind and the germ being of a spiritual nature, the husk or corn, and the nature or physical condition, being physical forces, see? Then, as the corn dies, the process is as the growth is seen in that as expressed to the entity, and the entity expressing same, see—that death, as commonly viewed, is not that of the passing away, or becoming a non-entity, but the phenomenized condition in a physical world that may be understood with such an illustration, viewed from the fourth-dimension viewpoint or standpoint, see?

Reading 140-10

The spiritual forces, in the spiritual consciousness, are cognizant of the condition in a physical plane until the spiritual has left that plane.

Reading 900-426

Life, in its continuity, is that experience of the soul or entity—including its soul, its spirit, its superconscious, its subconscious, its physical consciousness, or its *material* consciousness, in that as its *development* goes through the various experiences takes on more and more that ability of knowing itself to be itself, yet a portion of the great whole, or the one Creative Energy that is in and through all.

Reading 938-1

Life and its expressions are one. Each soul or entity will and does return, or cycle, as does nature in its manifestations about man; thus leaving, making or presenting—as it were—those infallible, indelible truths that it—Life—is continuous. And though there may be a few short years in this or that experience, they are one; the soul, the inner self being purified, being lifted up, that it may be one with that first cause, that first purpose for its coming into existence.

And though there may be those experiences here and there, each has its relationships with that which has gone before, that is to come. And there has been given to each soul that privilege, that choice, of being one with the Creative Forces. And the patterns that have been set as marks along man's progress are plain. *None* mount higher than that which has been left in Him who made that intercession for man, that man through Him might have the advocate with the Father. And those truths, those tenets—yea, those promises—that have been set in Him, are true; and may be the experience of each and every soul, as each entity seeks, strives, tries, desires to become and pursues the way of becoming one with Him.

For the words that He has given are simple, "Inasmuch as ye do it unto the least, ye do it unto me."

Then, as there has been and is the passage of a soul through time and space, through this and that experience, it has been and is for the purpose of giving more and more opportunities to express that which justifies man in his relationships one with another; in mercy, love, patience, long-suffering, brotherly love.

For these be the fruits of the spirit, and they that would be one with Him must worship Him in spirit and in truth.

Reading 1353-1

As Life is continuous, then the soul finds itself both in eternity and in spirit; in mind, yet in materiality.

If these become confused by the desires of self-aggrandizement or self-indulgence, or the glory of self for fame, for fortune or any of those that are considered as ideal conditions in a material plane, then the entity becomes confused.

But as has been indicated, if there is the continuous use of spiritual force, spiritual value in relationships to the mental and material, there is harmony, peace, understanding and wisdom in the knowledge of the divinity within.

As to those influences then that arise in the emotional self from the material sojourns, or those appearances in the material plane, not all of these are given, but those that are influencing—or that have their bearing upon the activities of the entity in the immediate or in the present sojourn, and how they may be used as constructive forces.

For unless a knowledge of a condition or experience is to be used as a practical application in the present, it becomes null and void as to constructive forces.

Reading 1474–1

Life is continuous! There is no halting.

Reading 1554–2

Life is continuous, and is Infinite!

Then, the retardment or advancement of each soul—as this entity—depends upon how well it comprehends or applies its understanding.

But it is a cycle, and continuously is an entity meeting itself.

Reading 1567–2

First we begin with the fact that God is; and that the heavens and the earth, and all nature, declare this. Just as there is the longing within every heart for the continuity of life.

What then is life? As it has been given, in Him we live and move and have our being. Then He, God, is! Or Life in all of its phases, its expressions, is a manifestation of that force or power we call God, or that is called God.

Then Life is continuous. For that force, that power which has brought the earth, the universe and all the influences in same into being, is a continuous thing—is a first premise.

All glory, all honor then, is due that creative force that may be manifested in our experiences as individuals through the manner in which we deal with our fellow man!

Then we say, when our loved ones, our heart's desires are taken from us, in what are we to believe?

This we find is only answered in that which has been given as His promise, that God hath not willed that any soul should perish but hath with every temptation, every trial, every disappointment made a way of escape or for correcting same. It is not a way of justification only, as by faith, but a way to know, to realize that in these disappointments, separations, there comes the assurance that He cares!

For to be absent from the body is to be present with that consciousness that we, as an individual, have worshiped as our God! For as we do it unto the least of our brethren, our associates, our acquaintance, our servants day by day, so we do unto our Maker!

What is the purpose then, we ask, for our entering into this vale, or experience, or awareness, where disappointments, fears, trials of body and of mind appear to mount above all of the glories that we may see?

In the beginning, when there was the creating, or the calling of individual entities into being, we were made to be the companions with the Father-God.

Now flesh and blood may not inherit eternal life; only the spirit, only the purpose, only the desire may inherit same.

Then that error in individual activity—not of another but of ourselves, individually—separated us from that awareness.

Hence God prepared the way through flesh whereby all phases of spirit, mind and body might express.

The earth then is a three-dimensional, a three-phase or three-manner expression. Just as the Father, the Son, the Holy Spirit are one. So are our body, mind and soul one—in Him.

Now we have seen, we have heard, we know that the Son represents or signifies the Mind.

He, the Son, was in the earth-earthy even as we—and yet is of the Godhead.

Hence the Mind is both material and spiritual, and taketh hold on that which is its environ, its want, in our experiences.

Then Mind, as He, was the Word—and dwelt among men; and we beheld Him as the face of the Father.

So is our mind made, so does our mind conceive—even as He; and *is* the Builder.

Then that our mind dwells upon, that our mind feeds upon, that do we supply to our body—yes, to our soul!

Hence we find all of these are the background, as it were, for the interpreting of our experience, of our sojourns in the earth.

For the astrological or the relative position of the earth (our immediate home) is not the center of the universe, is not the center of our thought; but the kingdom of the Father or the kingdom of Heaven is within! Why? Because our mind, the Son, is within us.

Then with that consciousness of His awareness, we may know even as He has given, "Ye abide in me, as I in the Father—I will come and abide with thee."

In that consciousness, then, the purposes for which each soul enters materiality are that it may become aware of its relationships to the Creative Forces or God; by the material manifestation of the things thought, said, *done*, in relation to its fellow man!

As the earth then occupies its three-dimensional phase of experience in our own solar system, and as each of those companions that are about the solar system represents as it were one of the phases of our conscience—the elements of our understanding—or our senses; then they each in their place, in their plane, bear a relationship to us, even as our desires for physical sustenance; that is: foods for the body; with all of the attributes, all of the abilities to take that we feed upon and turn it into elements for our body.

All of the elements are gathered from that upon which we have fed to build blood, bone, hair, nails; the sight, the hearing, the touching, the feelings, the expressions.

Why? Because these are *quickened* by the presence of the spirit of the Creative force (within).

So our mind, with its attributes, gathers from that upon which we feed in our mental self; forming our concepts of our relationship with those things that are contrarywise to His biddings or in line with that Law which is all-inclusive; that is, the love of the Father, with our mind, our body, our soul, and our neighbor as self.

Then all of these influences astrological (as known or called) from without, bear witness—or *are* as innate influences upon our activity, our sojourn through any given experience. Not because we were born with the sun in this sign or that, nor because Jupiter or Mercury or Saturn or Uranus or Mars was rising or setting, but rather:

Because we were made for the purpose of being companions with Him, a little lower than the angels who behold His face ever yet as heirs, as joint heirs with Him who *is* the Savior, the Way, then we have brought these about *because* of our activities through our *experiences* in those realms! Hence they bear witness by being *in* certain positions—because of our activity, our sojourn in those environs, in relationships to the universal forces of activity.

Hence they bear witness of certain urges in us, not beyond our will but controlled by our will!

For as was given of old, there is each day set before us life and death, good and evil. We choose because of our natures. If our will were broken, if we were commanded to do this or that, or to become as an automaton, our individuality then would be lost and we would only be as in Him without conscience—*conscience*—(consciousness) of being one with Him; with the abilities to choose for self!

For we *can*, as God, say Yea to this, Nay to that; we *can* order this or the other in our experience, by the very gifts that have been given or appointed unto our keeping. For we are indeed as laborers, co-laborers in the vineyard of the Lord—or of they that are fearful of His coming.

And we choose each day *whom* we will serve! And by the records in time and space, as we have moved through the realms of His kingdom, we have left our mark upon same.

Then they influence us, either directly or indirectly, in the manner as we have declared ourselves in favor of this or that influence in our material experience. And by the casting of our lot in this or that direction, we bring into our experience the influence in that manner.

2

●

God's Other Door

Reading 1472-2

Q: Does death instantly end all feeling in the physical body? If not, how long can it feel?

A: This would be such a problem; dependent upon the character of which unconsciousness is produced to the physical reaction—or the manner in which the consciousness has been trained.

Death—as commonly spoken of—is only passing through God's other door. That there is continued consciousness is evidenced, ever, by the associations of influences, the abilities of entities to project or to make those impressions upon the consciousness of sensitives or the like.

As to how long—many an individual has remained in that called death for what ye call *years* without realizing it was dead!

The feelings, the desires for what ye call appetites are changed, or not aware at all. The ability to communicate is that which usually disturbs or worries others.

Then, as to say how long—that depends upon the entity.

For as has been given, the psychic forces of an entity are *constantly* active—whether the soul-entity is aware of same or not. Hence as has been the experience of many, these become as individual as individualities or personalities are themselves.

Q: If cremated, would the body feel it?

9

A: What body?

The physical body is not the consciousness. The consciousness of the physical body is a separate thing. There is the mental body, the physical body, the spiritual body.

As has so oft been given, what is the builder? *mind*! Can you burn or cremate a mind? Can you destroy the physical body? Yes, easily.

To be absent (what is absent?) from the body is to be present with the Lord, or the universal consciousness, or the ideal. Absent from what? What absent? Physical consciousness, yes.

As to how long it requires to lose physical consciousness depends upon how great are the *appetites* and desires of a physical body!

Reading 2174–2

In Him, the Christ, as manifested in Jesus, ye find this—the first, the greatest commandment—"Thou shalt love the Lord thy God (that as manifested in self *as* life itself), and thy neighbor as thyself."

That which brings these both in awareness is that so well and yet so badly named *love*. God is love. An individual entity, each soul, each entity, each body, finds the need of expressing that called love in the material experience; from its first awareness until its last call through God's other door—the need of love, expressed, manifested, by self and from others.

As ye sow, so shall ye reap—this again becomes the foundation of what self, as well as others, may expect. If ye would have friends, show thyself friendly; if ye would have love, love ye one another. These are unchangeable. They do not alter. Man alters them only in the application—as to whether it is to satisfy the ego or the animal, or the flesh, or the mind.

These expressions, then, to self, as is experienced in motherhood, give the greatest glory manifested in the earth.

Reading 2927–1

Q: What journeys should I take for pleasure, which would be most interesting to me in this life?

A: These should be chosen from the promptings of that as would be contributory to meeting some of the hobbies of the entity, and in its relationship to the general contribution of knowledge to the universal activity.

Let that mind be in thee which was in Him, who gave, "I and the Father, God, are one." So become ye in thine own mind, as ye contribute, as ye attune thy inner self to those greater ideals; for it is not all of life just to live, nor yet all of death to die. For, they that put their whole trust in Him have passed from death unto life. And to such there is no death, only the entrance through God's other door.

Reading 3954-1

Yea, pray oft for those who have passed on. This is part of thy consciousness. It is well. For, God is God of the living. Those who have passed through God's other door are oft listening, listening for the voice of those they have loved in the earth. The nearest and dearest thing they have been conscious of in earthly consciousness. And the prayers of others that are still in the earth may ascend to the throne of God, and the angel of each entity stands before the throne to make intercession. Not as a physical throne, no; but that consciousness in which we may be so attuned that we become one with the whole in lending power and strength to each entity for whom ye speak and pray.

For, where two or three are gathered together in His name, He is in the midst of them. What meaneth this? If one be absent from the body, He is present with His Lord. What Lord? If you have been the ideal, that one to whom another would pay homage, you are then something of the channel, of the ideal. Then thy prayers direct such an one closer to that throne of love and mercy, that pool of light, yea that river of God.

Reading 5749-3

Q: Discuss the various phases of spiritual development before and after reincarnation in the earth.

A: This may be illustrated best in that which has been sought through example in the earth.

When there was in the beginning a man's advent into the plane known as earth, and it became a living soul, amenable to the laws that govern the plane itself as presented, the Son of man entered earth as the first man. Hence the Son of man, the Son of God, the Son of the first

Cause, making manifest in a material body.

This was not the first spiritual influence, spiritual body, spiritual manifestation in the earth, but the first man—flesh and blood; the first carnal house, the first amenable body to the laws of the plane in its position in the universe.

For, the earth is only an atom in the universe of worlds!

And man's development began through the laws of the generations in the earth; thus the development, retardment, or the alterations in those positions in a material plane.

And with error entered that as called *death*, which is only a transition—or through God's other door—into that realm where the entity has builded, in its manifestations as related to the knowledge and activity respecting the law of the universal influence.

Hence the development is through the planes of experience that an entity may become one *with* the first cause; even as the angels that wait before the Throne bring the access of the influence in the experience through the desires and activities of an entity, or being, in whatever state, place or plane of development the entity is passing.

For, in the comprehension of no time, no space, no beginning, no end, there may be the glimpse of what simple transition or birth into the material is; as passing through the other door into another consciousness.

Death in the material plane is passing through the outer door into a consciousness in the material activities that partakes of what the entity, or soul, has done with its spiritual truth in its manifestations in the other sphere.

Hence, as there came the development of that first entity of flesh and blood through the earth plane, he became *indeed* the Son—through the things which He experienced in the varied planes, as the development came to the oneness with the position in that which man terms the Triune.

Q: *Describe some of the planes into which entities pass on experiencing the change called death.*

A: Passing from the material consciousness to a spiritual or cosmic, or outer consciousness, oft does an entity or being not become conscious of that about it; much in the same manner as an entity born into the material plane only becomes conscious gradually of that designated as time and space for the material or third dimensional plane. In the passage the entity becomes conscious, or the recognition of being in a fourth or higher dimensional plane takes place, much in the same way as the consciousness is gained in the material.

For, as we have given, that we see manifested in the material plane is but a shadow of that in the spiritual plane.

In materiality we find some advance faster, some grow stronger, some become weaklings. Until there is redemption through the acceptance of the law (or love of God, as manifested through the Channel or the Way), there can be little or no development in a material or spiritual plane. But all must pass under the rod, even as He—who entered into materiality.

Reading 262–52

Q: Explain how so called good and evil forces are one.

A: This has just been explained. When there is delegated power to a body that has separated itself from the spirit (or coming from the unseen into the seen, or from the unconscious into the physical consciousness, or from God's other door—or opening from the infinite to the finite), then the activity is life; with the will of the source of that which has come into being. As to what it does with or about its associations of itself to the source of its activity, as to how far it may go afield, depends upon how high it has attained in its ability to throw off both negative and positive forces.

Hence we say, "The higher he flies the harder the fall." It's true!

Then, that which has been separated into the influence to become a body, whether celestial, terrestrial, or plain clay manifested into activity as man, becomes good or bad. The results to the body so acting are dependent and independent [interdependent?] (inter-between, see) upon what he does with the knowledge of—or that source of—activity.

Reading 390–2

Q: Would it be better if I gave up all thoughts of marriage and children?

A: The opportunity will come; for, to build the home—those that make for the cherishing and directing of the lives of those that may be lent to a union of love in the body—is to be a handmaid to the Creator.

For, the home becomes—to such that conduct their lives in that direction—as an outer door to the heavenly home.

For, as man and woman pass through God's other door from experience to experience, those that have been directed by thine hand will make for the blessings of the efforts put forth in the home.

Reading 1246-2

Q: Must I go on living?

A: Life is eternal. It is in Him, and merely to change through God's other door has only changed the outlook. But as we prepare the self for the vistas of the various consciousness upon the stages of development, we become a part of that—if our pathway is being led aright.

Q: What should my next step be in order to be of service to one and meet my financial obligations?

A: These become rather conflicting in their import, but know—O child of light—the earth is the Lord's and the fulness thereof, "The silver and the gold are mine, saith the Lord." *He* knoweth what thou hast need of. Be willing to put thy service to thy fellow man, thy service in a commercial world, into His hand. For God *alone* giveth the true increase. *Fear not*, if ye are in the Lord's hands! Fear rather if ye have slipped from same.

Reading 262-57

Q: Does the truth, "By becoming aware in a material world was the only manner through which spiritual forces might become aware of their separation from spiritual surroundings" show that the reincarnation of those who die in childhood is necessary?

A: As the awareness comes by separation (which is being manifested in materiality as we know it in the present), there is the necessity of the sojourning in *each* experience for the developments of the influences necessary in each soul's environ, each soul's attributes, to become again aware of being in the *presence* of the Father. Hence the reincarnation into this or that influence, and those that are only aware of material or carnal influences for a moment may be as *greatly* impressed as were a finite mind for a moment in the presence of Infinity. How long was the experience of Saul in the way to Damascus? How long was the experience of Stephen as he saw the Master standing—not sitting, *standing*? How long was the experience of those that saw the vision that beckoned to them, or any such experience?

When one considers the birth of a soul into the earth, the more often is the body and the body-mind considered than the soul—that is full-grown in a breath. For, did the Father (or Infinity) bring the earth, the worlds into existence, how much greater is a day in the house of the Lord—or a moment in His presence—than a thousand years in carnal forces?

Hence a soul even for a flash, or for a breath, has perhaps experienced even as much as Saul in the way.

3

●

More to Living and Dying Than We Realize

Reading 1977-1

As has been given, it is not all of life to live, nor yet all of death to die. For life and death are one, and only those who will consider the experience as one may come to understand or comprehend what peace indeed means.

Reading 2399-1

It isn't all of life to live, in one experience. For, life is continued; life itself is a consciousness, a gift of an infinite influence we may call God.

Thus does man comprehend that, it is in Him one lives and moves and has one's being; and that we as individuals may be coworkers with Creative Forces or God, or we may become egotists and thus magnify self and self's own abilities, self's own purposes, to such measures as to become at variance to those creative forces. Thus we shut ourselves away from the real birthright of each soul—that is, to know its relationships to this creative force or energy, and the manners or means of manifesting same by and through its daily relationships with the fellowmen.

Reading 2147-1

There is no death when the *entity* or the real self is considered; only the change in the consciousness of being able to make application in the sphere of activity in which the entity finds self.

Reading 2397-1

It is not all of life to live, nor yet all of death to die. For, each experience is by and through the grace of Him, the Giver of all that is good, all that is perfect; that His will may be made manifest in the purposes, the hopes, the ideals of each entity. For, He hath not willed that any soul should perish, but hath with each temptation prepared a way, a manner through which each soul may become aware of its faults, its virtues; magnifying the virtues, minimizing the faults—that one may come to the perfect knowledge of one's relationships to the creative influences—called God.

Reading 2842-2

If one will but take that ensample as was set in Him who made himself of no estate that He might gain the more. Using, then, this life as an ensample, one may apply—even as *this* entity may apply—these conditions in the earth's experience and develop toward that mark of higher calling as is set in Him—for it is not all of life to live, nor all of death to die; for one is the beginning of the other, and in the midst of life one is in the midst of death—in death one begins in that birth into which the *earthly* application of the inmost intents and desires has been applied in respect to will's forces, that given by the Creative Energy, that one might make self equal with that Energy.

Reading 2954-1

It is not all of life just to live, neither is it all of fame or fortune; for you have to live with yourself a long, long while.

Reading 2730-1

Keep the oneness of purpose; yet let *these* conditions ever be mindful to the entity: That it is not all of life to build material, nor all of death to die—in the high or low position, social, political or financial—but rather live the full life, ever being in that position of never asking anyone to do that which self would be ashamed for the mother to see self do.

Reading 3420-1

There is ever set before this entity daily (as each entity), good and evil, life and death. Life is growth. Death is as that separation or turning about, turning away from, or the opposite of growth.

Reading 1595-1

For as given of old, there is each day the *opportunity*. There is each day before thee life and death, good and evil.

Then know that there is oft a way which seemeth right unto a man, but the end thereof is death; death meaning in *this* sense confusion, disturbance, unstableness, unhappiness, and those things that go to make up such influences in the experience.

Reading 1432-1

But know the truth of that which was taught by those priests whom ye heard of old, and those upon whom you made many stripes for the announcing of their faith (or had it done) that "The Lord thy God is *one*!" Know that their law is true. While life and death are the opposites, they are constant companions one with another. Only the destructive forces know death as lord. Only spiritual or creative forces know life *as* the Lord. Know *ye* the Lord!

Reading 254-17

For God is Spirit and they that worship Him must worship in spirit and in truth, and as has been made manifest in the flesh with all power, all knowledge. As has been said, man must overcome through the knowledge and association of that knowledge with God's word made manifest in the flesh. The last to be overcome is death, and the knowledge of life is the knowledge of death. See? Any who may seek knowledge is seeking the greatest gifts of the gods of the universe, and in using such knowledge to worship God renders a service to fellow-man . . .

Reading 2282-1

Know that these are in keeping. Be thou faithful unto that time when ye may be called into the broader, the greater service. For there is not death, to those who love the Lord; only the entering into God's other chamber . . .

Hence in material manifestation the entity finds an interest in things and conditions that may be spoken of as concerning psychic or spiritual things. Let the greater interpretation of the word psychic to the self, to the souls of men, be rather as the soul forces of men than their disincarnate beings! For, as ye live and move and have thy being in and through the grace of the Creator, so may it indeed be true that whether ye live or whether ye pass into the other chambers of God's universe, ye are indeed His!

Keep ever before thee, then, the realization that "I am His; He is mine—if I keep His ways bright before my fellowmen."

These are the promises, then, which He so easily and so well gave, "If ye love me, ye will keep my commandments, and I and the Father will come and abide with thee. Lo, I am with you always, even unto the ends of the world."

It is not the end, then, because we pass from one room to another, from one consciousness to another. For, so is it proclaimed in that promise. Though we live in the physical consciousness, we pass—as this entity has oft—into those consciousnesses of Venus, Mercury, Jupiter, Uranus; for these are but stepping stones to the greater consciousness which He would have each soul attain in its relationships with and usage of its fellowmen.

Reading 3357-1

We find that the astrological aspects mean little to the entity, yet they each have their place, which—as indicated—is relative. No urge exceeds the will of the individual entity, that gift from and of the Creative Forces that separates man, even the Son of man, from the rest of creation. Thus it is made to be ever as one with the Father, knowing itself to be itself and yet one with the Father, never losing its identity. For, to lose its identity is death indeed—death indeed—separation from the Creative Force. The soul may never be lost, for it returns to the One Force, but knows not itself to be itself any more.

Reading 2823–1

Each entity is a part of the universal whole. All knowledge, all under-standing that has been a part of the entity's consciousness, then, is a part of the entity's experience.

Thus the unfoldment in the present is merely becoming aware of that experience through which the entity—either in body or in mind—has passed in a consciousness.

Hence there are two phases, or two means of expression from which urges arise in the experience of the entity. There is the form of con-sciousness attained when absent from the body, whether in normal sleep or in that sleep called death (in the earth plane). Then there is the consciousness to the soul-entity.

For, the entity finds itself body-physical, body-mind, body-soul. The body-soul is a citizen of that realm we call heaven, as much as the body-physical is a citizen of the land we call home.

These are the forms or the premises, then, through which influences arise.

Reading 900–370

. . . all life is one life, and the transition, the separation, the division, is as that given, so that even to man's sensuous consciousness the change takes place; yet each possession possessing the power, even as *in* the drop of water separated, or as water congealed or expanded has its own peculiar power through the various stages of transition. Each force as manifested in the various stages, or states, being as that illustration of the various stages a life may manifest in its varied forms, either be-fore combined in hydrogen and oxygen becoming water. Then in .a normal state representing a certain element separated by contact—cold or heat—changing form, and yet in each possessing a power, a force, all individual in itself, and only accessible when in *that* peculiar state.

Reading 136–18

We see in the physical world the condition in every form of life. As is taken here: We find a grain of corn or wheat that germ that, set in motion through its natural process with Mother Earth and the elements about same, brings forth corn *after its kind*, see? the kind and the germ being of a spiritual nature, the husk or corn, and the nature or physical condition, being physical forces, see? Then, as the corn dies, the process is as the growth is seen in that as expressed to the entity., and the entity expressing same, see—that death, as commonly viewed, is not that of the passing away, or becoming a non-entity, but the phenomenized condition in a physical world that may be understood with such an illustration, viewed from the fourth-dimension viewpoint or standpoint, see?

Reading 989-2

The earth's sojourns also make for such close associations with why the entity from one realm of experience to another experiences the entering of those realms from the application of the entity, as we have indicated, in each earthly realm.

Then, a death in the flesh is a birth into the realm of another experience, to those who have lived in such a manner as not to be bound by earthly ties. This does not mean that it does not have its own experience about the earth, but that it has lived such a *fullness* of life that it must be about its business.

Reading 5005-1

Do spiritualize thy purposes, thy ideals. For it is not all of life to live nor yet all of separation of the body to die. For to be absent from the body is to be present with thy God. What is thy God? Place, position in the earth? These are naught when things of the earth may not be used. For man enters the earth with a body prepared by others before him. He leaves the earth with the body-soul he has prepared for that realm of the interbetween, and can only depend, then, upon self according to that done with Creative Forces or God's laws. For they are perfect and are unchangeable.

Reading 5729-1

Astrological urges have become less and less a portion of the entity, for not merely material things but the controlling of material things has become the deeper urge for this entity. Hence the appearances in the earth and those that have a particular influence in the present are indicated, that the entity may take warning. Know that it isn't all of life to live. Neither is it all of life merely to make a success socially or financially. It is not satisfying to the soul, any more than the taking of thought will gratify the appetites or longings of nature in the body itself. These must have their answer one in and with another.

Reading 254–92

For do not consider for a moment (for this might be carried on to an indefinite end) that an individual soul-entity passing from an earth plane as a Catholic, a Methodist, an Episcopalian, is something else because he is dead! He's only a dead Episcopalian, Catholic or Methodist. And such personalities and their attempts are the same; only that *ideal*! For all are under the law of God equal, and how did He say even as respecting the home? "They are neither married nor given in marriage in the *heavenly* home but are *one!*"

Reading 1391–1

Yet if we learn more and more that separations are only walking through the rooms as it were of God's house, we become in these separations, in these experiences—aware of what is meant by that which has been and is the law, as from the beginning; "Know O ye peoples, the Lord thy God is *one!*"

And ye must be one—one with another, one with Him—if ye would be, as indeed ye are, corpuscles in the *life flow* of thy Redeemer!

Reading 497–1

For, life is of the Creator—and it may only be changed, it *cannot* be ended or destroyed. It can *only* return from whence it came. As to how soon it prepares its soul, that is of the influences that may be carried to the Maker, depends upon what that soul in its environs, in its experiences, does concerning that it knows about that He, the Father, would have it do.

There is not more required than can be fulfilled in the experience of any soul. It is true that others, and individuals, may make for influences that may make for changes in the activities, but if the ideal and the soul's longing is set in Him—only self may separate that soul from its Maker.

Reading 2911-1

Then, keep the mental attitude in that way of knowing in what there is life, light and immortality. It is not all of death to die, nor all of life to live. When there is sought that peace with Him, this may be had. For His promises are sure.

Reading 335-2

What *are* the ideals? What *are* the purposes and aims? What are the desired positions of the body, when analyzed by self? Just the accumulation of power, money, the position that comes with the accumulation of moneys? *Never*—or never altogether, in the basic thought of the individual—has this been true! Rather has it been builded that the necessity of having that power, or that which creates that power, is the basis of the *ideals* of the inner man!

It is well that the body take this into consideration, then, at this time when changes are probable, when conditions are such in the present associations that the activities, much that the body would have set, or the position the body would occupy (that is, by desire), may bring discontent, fear, an unsatisfactory feeling from within; for it is not yet all of life *just* to live, neither all of death to die!

Reading 2034-1

. . . there are the needs for the entity to analyze self, self's purpose, self's desire; realizing that it is not all of life to live, nor yet all of death to die, but that the expression of life is a creative thing, a creative influence or force in the experience, and that there must be an ideal; ideal spiritually, ideal mentally.

Thus there are the needs for the constructive thinking, rather than that as may be a hit or miss, or a haphazard study of conditions.

Reading 3343-1

In analyzing the urges, there is the great tendency for the entity to judge according to material standards, and to depend mentally upon physical manifestations. These are well, but—with such standards and with such a measuring stick—one may easily deceive self. For we are warned that there is a way that seemeth right to a man but the end thereof is death. Death is separation, lost opportunity—in some sphere of activity in which there is a consciousness, either spiritual or material. Mind is ever the builder, for it is the companion of soul and body, and is the way that is demonstrated and manifested in the earth in the Christ.

Reading 2630-1

Thus the outcome of any development, any retardment, is according to the use the entity makes of opportunities, and the ideal with which the entity entertains those opportunities.

It is not all of life, then, to live, nor all of death to die; but what the entity does *with* the opportunities as they present themselves.

Reading 136-70

Life is real, life is earnest! yet it is not all of life to live, nor all of death to die—for with the thoughts and the deeds done in the mind and the body, these are that builded by the entity, or body, and must be met, and an account given of those things rendered in the body and the mind. For the soul liveth, and is a portion of the Creative Energy, and it returns to the Whole, yet reserving in itself that oneness in the ability to know itself individual, yet a portion of the Whole. What manner of man would one be that would make of that Whole its own concept, other than one with the Whole?

Reading 2438-1

In analyzing self, learn that it is not all of life to merely live, or to supply the needs of the body—in materiality. For, life is a continuous thing, an expression of Divine; and the stamp of mind upon the self is the expression of love of that Divine for the companionship of the soul as an individual, as an entity.

Reading 1759-1

Each entrance of an entity into a material experience is that it may better fit itself, through the application of an ideal in its experience, for a sojourn with that which is Creative—that influence or force in which *all* move and have their consciousness, their being.

Then, unless the ideal as set as the standard of an entity in any given experience is of a creative force or nature, and takes hold upon that which is constructive and creative, what *must* the experience be when the soul has shed material consciousness, and as it stands before its own conscience, its God, *bare!*

There is in the material experience that which is ever as a manifestation of that excuse of old [Genesis?], "I was aware that I was naked and hence I covered myself with leaves." What are *Thy* excuses? What are thy conditions in thy activity, wherewith ye may stand as one that has sown the seed of righteousness? What is thy ideal of righteousness? Know that these can only be answered within thine own self. For thy body-physical is indeed the temple, the tabernacle of the living God; and there He hath promised to meet thee. For as the Teacher of teachers gave, the *kingdom* of heaven is *within thee!* and as ye make within thine own consciousness, through thy dwelling upon the thoughts of Him who is the Way, who is the Truth, who is the Light. And as He was asked in days just passed, "Speak to my brother, that he divide the inheritance with me." His answer came, "Who made me to be a judge between thee and thy brother?

Reading 2080–1

These then are chosen—these urges that are indicated good and bad—that there may be an analyzing of self; that the entity may realize that it is not all of life just to live, and to enjoy the good things of material experience.

For thou art indeed thy brother's keeper. There are those opportunities ever being presented for the real abilities which are within the experience and the consciousness of the entity. In taking advantage of, or using, such opportunities in the proper direction, the entity may make his paths straight, and know the purposes for which each soul enters a material experience; that these are not just that ye may have to hold, other than as a keeper of opportunities in hope, in love, in faith, in patience, as unto thy Maker.

It is not sufficient, then, to merely live that ye may outwardly appear as a successful individual—not too bad nor too good but to be one who, irrespective of others, chooses the better place.

Reading 3436-2

This information should be, then, as a .helpful influence if the entity will but analyze self, self's abilities and the desires and hopes for the entity. Do *not*, then, allow self to become so material-minded that the judgments are measured only by the material yardstick of material accomplishments. For what profiteth a man who does gain the whole world and loseth his own soul? Or what would ye gain in exchange for the awareness of thy soul, that ye may know life is indeed eternal; and it isn't then all of life to live, nor all of death to die.

Reading 4400-1

There is also that necessity for the individual to so attune self from the spiritual effect that must be instilled in the individual *to whom* such applications may be made, as would come under the supervision of the individual; for it is not *all* of life to live, nor yet all of death to die—for in the midst of death one is in the midst of life, and it behooves one, then, that their own individual life be such that it—their life—is compatible to those tenets, those teachings, those principles, as would be set up by the application of self's efforts toward the individuals whom one would attend.

Reading 5005-1

Do spiritualize thy purposes, thy ideals. For it is not all of life to live nor yet all of separation of the body to die. For to be absent from the body is to be present with thy God. What is thy God? Place, position in the earth? These are naught when things of the earth may not be used. For man enters the earth with a body prepared by others before him. He leaves the earth with the body-soul he has prepared for that realm of the inter-between, and can only depend, then, upon self according to that done with Creative Forces or God's laws. For they are perfect and are unchangeable.

Reading 2573-1

While it is not all of life to live, each soul enters for a purpose. And it is not merely to gain fame or fortune, nor to be thought well of in the material plane only; but it is a real spiritual and mental experience also.

Reading 2142–1

One that may be trusted in its relationships with others, and to its own sorrow has often found another's word is *not* as their bond; while for self that promised is to self as binding as were it a bond; though these must be often dissuaded in self. Well that self *keep* this same attitude; for as to those relationships, these make for that that will make life more worthwhile in business, social, political, economical, regions or sources of one's experience; for it is not *all* of life to live, nor yet all of death to die; for, as is builded in the experience of self, whether in the marital, the social, the political, the religious or the business associations, each and every individual becomes a reflection of that *that* individual holds as its ideal—whether that ideal be position, fame, fortune, or the aggrandizing of selfish interests, or self's own motives or bodily desires. These become paramount in the entity's *inner* self, and when these are builded upon that that is not of the ideal, they must sooner or later be wrecked upon those of discouragement, disorder, discontent, disconcerted activity, those of strained relations with friends, associates, family, and the like—for those that breed contempt must have the same as its own bedfellows.

Reading 670–1

. . . those things in which the judgments or activities of the entity may engage—either in the mental, material or spiritual ever must be governed by those things of a spiritual source or nature. For, as will ever be seen in any influence, the spirit is willing but the flesh is weak. The environs and hereditary influences that may be said to be from the purely material sense would never answer in the activities for this entity, whether in relationship to material or spiritual things, as an answer for that to which it would bring itself in relationships with or without these conditions. For the basis in this entity's experience must be that which is well-grounded in self from first taking counsel within self and knowing from what basis, from what standard the judgments of the activities are to be judged or governed; and these will make for the general assurance within the experiences that the outcome of whatever activity in which the entity may engage in the material sense will bring *for the* experience that which is worthwhile. For, it is not all of life alone

to live nor all of death to die, to those that have visioned—and do vision—that purpose for which the experience of an entity is engaged in
its passage through any particular experience in the earth.

Reading 4028-1

Q: Does the Doctor appreciate my putting flowers on his mothers grave?

A: This should not be as to whether the Doctor appreciates it or not.
Let it be an answer to thee, to the mother. For if this is done in the right
spirit, it will bring many more returns than if done purposely to please
someone living. This is not the gaining of something from same, but the
contributing to the memory, with the thought of love and compassion.

Reading 5122-1

Those activities of the entity should be in or around flowers. For this
entity has so oft been the music and the flower lady, until it becomes
second nature to work in or with those either in arranging bouquets or
corsages, or even the very foolish way of sending to those who have
passed on. They need the flowers when they are here, not when they
are in God's other room!

Reading 5155-1

Q: Will I overcome death in this incarnation?

A: There is no death. Death is only overcome by Him, who has overcome death. It is our promise, and when ye abide in Him sufficient to
that, ye with Him, as the resurrection, may indeed overcome death in a
material sense.

Reading 262-73

For He is the way; He is the life; He is the vine and ye are the branches.
Bear ye fruit, then, worthy of that thou hast chosen; and He will keep
that thou hast committed unto Him against every experience that may
be required, that may be needed, that may come in thine attempts to
show forth the Lord's death till He come again; Death meaning that
transition, that decision, that change in every experience. For if ye die
not daily to the things of the world ye are none of His.

Reading 3188-1

For, no soul enters any experience perchance. For it comes with a purpose. And the entity as well as every entity should know: The divine, the First Cause, is mindful of the entity. This is evidenced by the very fact that the entity finds itself conscious of being itself and aware of good and evil, light and darkness, life and death. These are all one. One is as life and death. There is no death to the spiritual. Hence by his passing through same, proved, indicated, that He overcame death; that we through Him might have *life* and life more abundant. These should be not merely tenets or truths for the entity, but living things, living experiences. . .

And again He has said, as He showed the way, as He fulfilled in giving his life, "In the day ye eat thereof ye shall surely die." Yet the tempter said, "Not surely die," for it may be put off; and it was —six hundred years—and yet death came, and pangs of the loss of self. Yet in that day when the voice was raised on the Cross, he said, "Father, why— why the way of the Cross?" This is indeed the pattern that is interpreted in "I perceive that the heart of man is to do evil—the spirit is willing, the flesh is weak."

Reading 262-13

The harvest indeed is ripe, the laborers are few! The Lords have called, do call, for laborers in His vineyard. *Who* will work today? He that has seen a vision of the love of Him that has been set as thine example, as thine ideal. These founded in those that are of man's making *must* come to naught! With the cooperation of the Spirit of Truth it is *made* alive in Him, even as the overcoming of death itself through the applying of self to *His* will. Not *my* will but thine, O Lord, be done in me! As the meditations should be, in the preparation of faith in self, in God, in thy ideal: "Create in me a pure heart, O God! Open Thou mine heart to the faith Thou hast implanted in all that seek Thy Face! Help Thou mine unbelief in my God, in my neighbor, in myself!"

Reading 2927-1

Let that mind be in thee which was in Him, who gave, "I and the Father, God, are one." So become ye in thine own mind, as ye contribute, as ye attune thy inner self to those greater ideals; for it is not all of life just to live, nor yet all of death to die. For, they that put their whole trust in Him have passed from death unto life. And to such there is no death, only the entrance through God's other door.

Reading 1152-1

But when the Prince of Peace came—into the earth for the completing of His *own* development in the earth, *He* overcame the flesh *and* temptation. So He became the first of those that overcame death in the body, enabling Him to so illuminate, to so revivify that body as to take it up again, even when those fluids of the body had been drained away by the nail holes in His hand and by the spear piercing His side.

Yet this body, this entity, *too*, may do these things; through those promises that were so new yet so old, as given by Him. "Not of myself do I these things," saith He, "but God, the Father that worketh in me; for I *come* from Him, I go to Him."

He came, the Master, in flesh and blood, even as thou didst come in flesh and blood. Yet as He then proclaimed to thee, there is a cleansing of the body, of the flesh, of the blood, in such measures that it may become illumined with power from on high; that is *within* thine own body to *will*! "Thy will, O God; not mine, but Thine, be done in me, through me."

This was the message as He gave when He; too, overcame; surrendering all power unto Power itself, surrendering all will unto the will of the Father; making of self then a channel through which others taking hope through the knowledge that He hath perfected Himself, may bring to thee that grace, that mercy, that is eternity with Him and in Him.

Reading 1158-5

Be patient—be patient, my child; for in patience know ye thine own soul and become aware that I am able to sustain thee, even though ye walk through the valleys and in the shadows of death." For death hath no sting, it hath no power over those that know the Resurrection, even as thou hath seen and as thou hast known, as thou hast heard, how the Resurrection brought to the consciousness of man that power that God hath given to man, that may reconstruct, resuscitate, even every atom

of a physically sick body, that may resurrect even every atom of a sin-
sick soul, may resurrect the soul that it lives on and on in the glory of a
resurrected, a regenerated Christ in the souls and hearts of men!

Reading 1158-9

Resurrection means what? It is reciprocal of that which has been
expressed. How hath it been put again by him whom ye knew but
disliked (for ye loved Peter the better)? "There is no life without death,
there is no *renewal* without the dying of the old." Dying is not blotting
out, it is transition—and ye may know transition by that as comes into
the experience by those very activities, that "With what message ye
mete it shall be measured to thee again." That was His life, that is thy
life, that is each one's life. Then how near, how dear has grown in the
hearts, in the minds of all, those who put away self that they may know
Him the better?

He put away self, letting it be nailed to the Cross; that the *new*, the
renewing, the fulfilling, the *being* the Law, becomes the Law!

For it is the Law to *be* the Law, and the *law* is Love! Even as He showed
in all of His manifestations, in the material experiences in the earth;
that ye doubted, honestly—that is in the eyes, in the heart, in the soul
even of the Creator counted—even as of old—desire, honest desire (not
because faults did not arise in material world but they were meted to
Abraham, even as He said)—as *faith*!

Faith is manifested by that evidence of things not seen, but the hope
in the promises of that which is Creative in thine inner self, thine own
soul, as it seeks expression, hopes for in the life, yea in the blood of the
Lamb which is the Life that lights the whole world!

Disposition of the Material Body—

Reading 275-29

Q: How should a body be prepared for burial?

A: This depends upon the development or that builded in the consciousness of the individual, as to what is necessary for the loosening of
the elementals from the physical body. As has been noted, this may
best be studied by the manner in which the various religious forces or

cults dispose of such bodies in India; for, as has been given, "Here we may know their belief, or what they think they believe, by the manner in which disposition is made of the body."

That that would be ideal is that it may be hermetically sealed, or by fire, or by the separation of the atmosphere from the body.

Q: *What is the best disposition of a body, for the sake of all?*

A: By fire!

Reading 1472-2

Q: *If cremated, would the body feel it?*

A: What body?

The physical body is not the consciousness. The consciousness of the physical body is a separate thing. There is the mental body, the physical body, the spiritual body.

As has so oft been given, what is the builder? *mind!* Can you burn or cremate a mind? Can you destroy the physical body? Yes, easily. To be absent (what is absent?) from the body is to be present with the Lord, or the universal consciousness, or the ideal. Absent from what? What absent? Physical consciousness, yes.

As to how long it requires to lose physical consciousness depends upon how great are the *appetites* and desires of a physical body!

Reading 378-11

Q: *Is a crematorium the best place to burn a dead body by fire?*

A: That depends, to be sure, upon the feelings or activities of an individual towards such dispositions. As we would find, the safer and the better way would be in such a place.

The Borderland, Where the Dead Transition—

Reading 262-89

They that are on the borderland are only in that state of transition.

Reading 1404-1

There are many influences and many forces, but only one *spirit* of good. There are many entities in the inter-between, in the borderland, in the shadowland, in the developing along the way; but only one spirit of truth, which is life everlasting!

Reading 900-10

Q: What is meant by the Borderland as referred to in a reading?

A: That condition that the living experience with the soul, the mental faculties, the desire, the consciousness of the various phases of each laid aside and the soul, with its companion, the sub-conscious, peeps into the interlay between the spirit and soul, or superconscious, or that existence as lies in that space where the impressions of the disincarnate spirits, with their soul, communicate with such earthly conditions as illustrated in this:

When the physical body lies in slumber, we find the organs that are subjugated, the life-giving flow and the subconscious forces acting, and the soul forces ready for that communication with intermingling conditions lying between.

Again, as in the present sphere, in this body lying here [Edgar Cayce], we find all life in suspension, only portions of the higher vibrations in accord with those vibrations that communicate with the Universal forces.

Reading 3976-3

Have some terribly hard times in China today. In the Manchurian region, a flood and fire both. Many peoples are passing into the Borderland, their entities taking their position as has been manifest through their environment in the earth plane at present time. There are those conditions arising from this great boredom in the consciousness of many that will bring the revolution in the minds of many peoples, and begin that understanding of the purpose of the Gift of God to the World in the One made manifest in the flesh, and able to bring the consciousness made manifest in the world to the peoples. Hence many will be able through this to lay aside the physical and again manifest in a physical before men.

Reading 900-346

There are many various phases of the operations of those in the

Borderland, and many types, many classes, many characters, that seek
the expression of that development found in the various entities who
may lay aside the physical for the operation of either that in the 4th
dimensional nature or that in the purely ultraistic [altruistic?] nature as
was manifested by that entity, who in the weeks ago passed into the
spirit plane. In the study of such, be thou well balanced in that thou
studyest [studiest], for know that those who seek more for the material
manifestation seeketh rather for the sign, and as the Master gave, no
sign shall be given to a wicked or adulterous generation.

Reading 900-8

Q: *How may this body attune his mind with that of his father who has gone from
this earth's sphere?*

A: Just as has been given. Study into the Borderland, as has been
given; with the study, the thought, the lapsing of the self into these
conditions, where the consciousness is laid aside and the superconsciousness rules, we may come into such communications, as this
body has in sleep. Not well that this be dwelt upon at all times, for we
bring to the other entity distresses at times.

Q: *This body was told to write in the third dream. What should he write?*

A: Those things he has been given the glimpse of in the Borderland,
or of those conditions that come from information that comes from
Borderland.

Q: *What is the interpretation of this Borderland he saw in his dream?*

A: The vision of the possibilities of gaining and understanding of
conditions that do exist, may exist, and will exist in the sub-conscious,
super-conscious or souls of individuals that live, have lived, may live in
earth's plane. This is, and should be considered, as the vision as of
Daniel.

Q: *Was this dream given to warn him of anything wrong he was doing?*

A: There is warning in all of these. Hence the last, "Study or look into
the Borderland." Nothing wrong toward the entity's personal actions,
save as the warning of the usage of the person's facilities and possibilities of developing for the Borderland.

Reading 900-328

Q: Morning of July 11th. Another of series on spirit communication, so called, that started with the experience of digging through the earth from the earth plane to cosmic, at tennis time. This heralded in this series of dreams, or predicted it. In this one I crossed the bridge of life that I have gone half way over before. As I landed on the other shore, the Voice spoke saying: "For the Association of National Investigators." Upon landing upon that shore I was conscious of a great noise, of a speeding up or quickening of activity. I felt a certain freedom. I was afraid on this Borderland that some earthly or evil spirits might control. My father spoke saying: "No, you reach beyond them. You are free to choose here, and you are under control. You command the entities of this plane." I felt a great power, and many about me. Much more that I will not describe here, came into my consciousness, but I felt a little of what my father had previously told me, as follows: "[900], you will never know your capacity to work for good while you are in the flesh, but when you come into the spirit then you will know." The buzzing sound grew louder. What was this? And the speed increased in rapidity, and as my senses became bewildered, [136's father] spoke to me saying: "[900], you know us," and I felt that I did.

A: This, as we see, is as given, the greater understanding to the entity as respecting the Borderland and its association with those in the spirit plane, or in the activity of the cosmic forces.

As is indicated in the crossing over on the bridge of life, the entity—through set definite purposes—finds self into that plane wherein there becomes specific action in the full manifestations of the *application* of truths understood and truths disseminated, and as is given to the entity, through those that remain near and dear to the inmost being of the body, the entity finds that in this definite way, in this definite stand taken, there is that assurance that there enters not that which may take from that builded by the entity toward the better knowledge and understanding.

In the increase of the noise, is as the raising of that vibration that exists between that of the material and the spiritual, and—as given by the father—there cannot be the full consciousness of the one without the laying aside of the other, for no one serves two masters.

In the knowledge of the presence of others comes the greater understanding of the great leveler that comes with the more perfect understanding of the one in all, and with the continuing of the great noise, as

is seen, there is the continual knowledge of the body, mentally, consciously, physically, being raised to that higher power, even as is set in
Him who gave, "And I, if I be lifted up, will draw all men unto me."

Keep thine self physically, mentally, spiritually, in the way of understanding, and in this new way, this new manner, draw others into that
light that brings the more perfect understanding of life lived worth
while, and the satisfying of the knowledge of oneness with the Father.

Reading 900-331

We have the body, the enquiring mind, and the dreams. These we
have had here before. The dreams, as we see, come through those chan-
nels as have been outlined to the entity, and again we find the entity
approaches closer and closer to the threshold of the Borderland in consciousness and in understanding. Hence there is seen more and more of
the reasoning from within toward the outward appearances of conditions, and the entity should in the quieter moments gain better understanding of the phases of life and of how the application of the lessons
and truths gained apply in the lives of others. Not to condemn, not to
bring railings on any, but that the love of the Father may be made
manifest in the earth—for, as the entity goes in and out among men,
and as truth, trust, love, and the kindred phases of life, enter into the
secular things of life, this—as is seen and experienced by the entity—
becomes the more worth while—and while the conditions of the secular
things may pass and fade, these—love, charity, long suffering, and such
kindred conditions—remain, and stand the test of so as by fire.

Prayer for Those Who Have Entered the Borderland—

Reading 281-15

Q: Please give a prayer for those who have passed on.

A: Father, in Thy love, Thy mercy, be Thou near those who are in—
and have recently entered—the borderland. May I aid, when Thou seest
that Thou canst use me.

4

●

The Dying and Dead Experience

Reading 5195-1

Yes, we have the body; and the soul would take leave of same. There are many experiences in a life's journey in the earth that are much more serious than that man calls death, when the trust of the soul and heart of the man is in the Lord, who doeth all things well. There is little interpretation-physical of the disturbance, and it is gradually progressing in the inabilities of the entity to do for self, think for self. Even yet there is in the consciousness the desire that those, for whom the entity has been responsible for their being in the earth, should take note and prepare while they may to meet their God.

For the time cometh, as it must to this body, when no work is to be done but ye must stand before the judgment bar of thine own conscience, as must each soul, and determine as to whether in the light of the knowledge, in the light of thine opportunity, ye can as thy friend, thy God say, "I have dishonored no man, 1 have taken naught from my brother, but what 1 restore fourfold."

And remember, as this entity goes to its long rest, there are those whom he has entrusted with an obligation. Do not disregard the counsel. For he has been and is viewing those past opportunities that soon shall come no more in this life. There are the warnings, heed them! For the Lord will not always smile on those who disregard the warnings

which have been and are being now, here, made to those whom this
body would have—heed the warning.

Reading 1408–2

Mrs. Cayce: You will have before you the circumstances and conditions surrounding the death of [1408], —, Penna., June 8, 1937; together
with the various members of her family and the questions resulting
from her sudden death; especially the questions of [her daughter], who
requests a Reading on these conditions. You will give that which may
be helpful to the family at this time and answer the questions which
they have presented.

Mr. Cayce: Yes, we have those circumstances and conditions attend-
ing the separation of the body and soul of [1408].

In giving that as would be helpful and constructive in the experience
of each member of this family:

As has been so aptly said, her life, her work, her love, is an example
of Christian faith and fortitude.

Hence for those that wait:

It would be selfish to wish or desire conditions to be different. For in
His Wisdom He hath seen fit to leave—in the love as was manifested in
the life—an example for each; in patience, in courage, in forbearance; in
keeping a watchful, careful attention on the lives of each of the family.

The body was so tired from the cares of the material world that the
physical reactions were in the heart; that had been so ready to open
itself to the needs of each, not only of the family but to all that know,
that even were acquainted with the body.

Yet it grew so weary with these cares that He, in His love, saw fit to let
the separation come; that the soul might in peace *rest* in the arms of
Him who is her Savior—Jesus!

Hence you each should take the lesson of that courage, of that patience, of that forbearance, of that long-suffering, as a part of *your* own
lives; and let it become—as she manifested—the *experience* of the every-
day life, in the dealings and in the associations with the fellowman.

The physical condition that wrought the change was the engorge-
ment of the arteries between the heart and the liver. The dregs of hard-
ships, of trials, became heavy.

As to the message that she would leave, that she would give to each:

To [269]: Keep a watchful eye upon [son], and keep the children together in their varied experiences; for in the union of purpose is there
strength for all.

To [1st daughter]: Keep the care that has been given thee, even as a
good shepherdess watching over the flock, even as He has shown in His
ways.

To [2nd daughter]: Care for the home. Let that be thy part, thy mission, now. When there are the changes that are natural to come, these
then will be a share of another; but keep thou the home for Papa, for
[son], for [Baby—4th daughter].

To [3rd daughter]: Let those things wherein oft reproved, oft directed,
be kept in that loving faith that has been thy outlook upon life. For
hold fast to the things that bespeak of the true spiritual life; for in these
ye find peace and happiness and joy.

To [son]: Attend thy father's needs. Be his right hand. If it is in keeping with thy inner self, prepare thy ways in the preparations in school
for the activities of life itself. But look after him.

To the baby: Let [3 older sisters], keep watchful care with thee. Know,
as is in the experience of those that have lived and know the pitfalls;
know those things that make one weary, but hold fast to that which is
good.

And may the blessings of the Father, through the love as shown in
the Christ, guide each of you. Through the vicissitudes of life, through
all the shadows, through all the disappointments, through all the sorrows, know He is near—and will hold thee by the hand.

Reading 4938-1

9/28/35 Miss [4938] fell out of her bedroom window at school and was killed.

Mrs. C: You will have before you the entity known as [4938], who was
in one of the dormitories at Barnard College, New York City, in the early
morning of Saturday, September 28th. You will tell us what you are
privileged to tell, and that which will be helpful to those closely concerned. You will then answer the questions that may be asked by her
aunt, present in this room.

Mr. C: Yes, we are with the entity here.

This, as may be and should be understood by those who are interested, was an accident—and not premeditated or purposed by the entity. The environs or surroundings that made for these happenings, in a material world, are with the entity in the present, making for better understandings. Those that are near and dear to the entity, to make for more understandings—condemn no one, nor the circumstance. Neither mourn for those that are at rest.

There is gradually coming the awakening. This, to be sure, is an experience through which the entity, [4938] is passing in the present. It is making for a helpfulness in its understanding and comprehending of that which is the experience, the awareness of same in the present.

The body–physical that was broken is now whole in Him.

Let thy prayer then be:

In Thy mercy, in Thy goodness, Father, keep her. Make for those understandings in my experience, in her experience, that we may draw nearer and nearer together in that oneness of purpose that His love is known more and more in the minds and the hearts of those that are in the positions of opportunities for being a channel, a messenger, in the name of the Christ. Amen.

Ready for questions.

Q: Is she happy, and does she understand where she is?

A: As given, there is the awakening, and there is the understanding coming more and more.

And soon to the Aunt may come the awareness of her presence near. These are the conditions.

Q: Is there anything any of us can do to help her in any way?

A: Let the prayer as given be held occasionally, especially in the early mornings.

Reading 1270–1

Mr. C: Yes, we have those conditions that surround this body, [1270].

As we find, these might have been helped in the beginnings of these; but the advanced condition is such that not only is there the involving of same into the blood stream so that there is the hardening of tissue but there is the evolving of tissue into the fluid waters.

So, only to keep the body as easy as possible, and to maintain about this developing mind the *beauty* of transition, is the help as we find that may be given.

A great deal might be given from the attitudes or phases of karmic forces, but for the material physical—to only make to the understanding mind the beauties of transition in the spiritual evolution of the mental and soul forces offers for the body and those about same that help, that stamina, that makes for a greater comprehending of the purposes of a soul's entrance into materiality, even though to suffer under those experiences and to bring—as it appears—little opportunity of material help.

Yet these experiences build into the warp and woof of each soul that which is a *continued* development for those that seek to know the ways of Divinity in its dealings with man. '

Hence let each study to show *themselves approved* unto the Creative Forces. While these appear from the material view as very little, the hope and the promise that have been given are sure—if we hold to those and claim them by our dealings with others as our very own.

Reading 5194-1

Yes, as we find, there is little materially that may be administered for any physical help in this present experience for this body.

There should be rather those administrations of the mental and spiritual help which may be given by those who are near and close to the entity who may apply such in their own lives to make easier that journey which this entity soon must take. For life is not spent just because changes come about, but the greater opportunity for this soul-entity is to be released from the suffering. For in the same manner as He, who is the way, suffered, so must each individual meet that in the flesh; that we may know that the Savior bears with each soul that which will enable life, consciousness, to be a continuous experience.

Thus it behooves those who seek help, even, to be patient, to be gentle, to be kind to others. For this entity needs not, save the assurance that those whom she holds near and dear will strive the harder to meet her again in that better understanding.

Reading 5344–1

EC: Yes, we have the body, [5344].

There has already been departure of the soul, which only waits by here. We have the physical being but the control of same only needs the care, the attention, the greater love which may be shown in and under the circumstances, which will give the best conditions for this body. For already there are those weakenings so of the centers of the cerebrospinal system that no physical help, as we find, may be administered, only the mental or soul help as will be a part of the mental or superconscious self.

This condition has come from pressures which caused dementia praecox.

Reading 1824–1

Too late in the application of those things for material benefits in this present experience. As is indicated, not only the toxic forces have been the more active but sepsis has already begun.

These then would rather be for those who are mindful of the associations and relations:

Know that life is a continuous experience, and as there is a consciousness in sleep that is not physical—in the sense of physical awareness—so there is a consciousness in the same manner when the physical is entirely laid aside.

He indeed is the resurrection and the life. In *Him* do we put our trust.

Then there should not be sorrow and sadness in those periods when the physical turmoils and strifes of the body are laid aside, for the moment, for the closer walk with Him.

For indeed to be absent from the material body is to be present with the Lord.

Let those admonitions and those promises, then, fill thy life and so determine within selves that ye will walk the closer with Him day by day.

And then when the shadows, as here, begin to close about, and there is the meeting at the river, there will be indeed no sorrow when this barque puts out to sea.

Reading 1567–2

Then we say, when our loved ones, our heart's desires are taken from us, in what are we to believe?

This we find is only answered in that which has been given as His promise, that God hath not willed that any soul should perish but hath with every temptation, every trial, every disappointment made a way of escape or for correcting same. It is not a way of justification only, as by faith, but a way to know, to realize that in these disappointments, separations, there comes the assurance that He cares!

For to be absent from the body is to be present with that consciousness that we, as an individual, have worshiped as our God! For as we do it unto the least of our brethren, our associates, our acquaintance, our servants day by day, so we do unto our Maker!

Reading 3954–1

Then fret not thyself over others, but keep the faith. Walk in the Way. Keep the lights burning ever, and others will find the Way who in the present appear to be far in arrears with appreciations of the glory and love of the heavenly Father.

Yea, pray oft for those who have passed on. This is part of thy consciousness. It is well. For, God is God of the living. Those who have passed through God's other door are oft listening, listening for the voice of those they have loved in the earth. The nearest and dearest thing they have been conscious of in earthly consciousness. And the prayers of others that are still in the earth may ascend to the throne of God, and the angel of each entity stands before the throne to make intercession. Not as a physical throne, no; but that consciousness in which we may be so attuned that we become one with the whole in lending power and strength to each entity for whom ye speak and pray.

For, where two or three are gathered together in His name, He is in the midst of them. What meaneth this? If one be absent from the body, He is present with His Lord. What Lord? If you .have been the ideal, that one to whom another would pay homage, you are then something of the channel, of the ideal. Then thy prayers direct such an one closer to that throne of love and mercy, that pool of light, yea that river of God.

Aiding in the Presence of Death—

Reading 1175-1

Q: How may I develop a spiritual consciousness, so as to make emotionally mine the belief that the so-called dead are alive; that my loved ones are near, loving me and ready to help me?

A: As has been given, know thy Ideal, in what thou hast believed; and then act in that manner, ministering to others. For perfect love casteth out fear, and fear can only be from the material things that soon must fade away.

And thus hold to the higher thought of *eternity*. For life is a *continual* experience. And thy loved ones, yea those thou hast loved. For what draweth thee nigh to others, to do a kindly deed; to pass a kindly word to those that are disconsolate, those that are in sorrow? It makes for a bond of sympathy, a bond of love that surpasseth all joy of an earthly nature. . .

Q: What more may I do to aid my husband?

A: Soon the passing must be. Hold fast to the strength in self, making for the harmony or the comfort or the joys that come through those little associations that mean for strength to both.

Reading 1059-1

Q: How long will he linger?

A: This depends upon those conditions as just intimated; that as soon as there is the breaking up again of the cellular forces, then the separations will begin. This will depend upon the vitality of the body, and the ability of the heart's action to work under the distresses and disorders that exist.

This may be eighteen to twenty-four days.

Q: Anything further for the body, or advice for his daughter—Mrs. [601]—who is with him?

A: There should not be the attempt upon the part of any in the material activities to make for distresses about the body. For these changes that come in the experience of the soul and spiritual activity of a body are the natural consequences. And these should be viewed from that ideal; that those forces which make for the greater construction should be kept in the spiritual manner for the body.

Reading 1786-2

Q: Have I any further contact with my late husband . . . since he has passed on?

A: If that is the desire, it will continue to hang on to same! If it is to be finished, and that which has been to be the development, then leave this aside.

Q: Does he know of my prayers?

A: Do you wish him to? Do you wish to call him back to those disturbing forces, or do you wish the self to be poured out for him that he may be happy? Which is it you desire—to satisfy self that you are communicating, or that you are holding him in such a way as to retard? or hast thou *believed* the promise? Leave him in the hands of Him who is the resurrection! Then prepare thyself for same.

Reading 1782-1

Q: Is it well to foster the sense of continued communication with his spirit while we are separated by "death," so-called?

A: If this is for a helpful experience to each, it is well. Let it rather be directed by that communion with Him who has promised to be *with* thee always; and hinder not then thy companion, but—in such associations and meetings—give the direction to the Holy One.

Reading 480-47

Q: Can you tell me what is the best approach through this channel for me to gain an understanding from the spiritual angle of the apparent tragedy which has come in my life through the loss of my mother?

A: The Lord giveth, the Lord taketh away. Such as these appear to come as trite sayings, but as we study the Scripture and the promises therein, we find that only does the answer come within the self. Know that as He *wills*, only that which is for the individual—for *all* concerned—the will of Him as it is done in each, able to make for that awakening necessary for the better understanding. Condemning of self, of others, of the lack of this or that or the other, only creates barriers that make for the *inability of* the self to catch the glimpse.

Read that which has been indicated in the last admonition of Moses, in the 30th of Deuteronomy. Read of those promises in the Psalms—as in the 24th, the 23rd, the 91st, the 1st, the 150th. All of these will indicate that which is the *source* of strength mentally and spiritually, and—if we coordinate our mental and physical selves—also the source of our body's strength. For, as indicated in those, the *source* of all is there.

If we look, then, for other means—or material means—for the answer, there is none. Only is it found in Him.

Reading 2401-1

Q: How can I best adjust myself to the passing of my husband, and carry on as I should?

A: As has been indicated [regarding her being lonesome, home sick, so few friends]—in the manners as we have outlined.

Keep close to that assurance that he *liveth!*

Reading 5488-1

Q: Is there any message you could give regarding her husband, who has passed beyond, that would help her?

A: These, as we may find, may best be had through that introspection of self in those periods when one may turn to the within and seek that counsel, that at-oneness with those who are in the borderland; for *all* is well in the oneness of the purposes as may be accomplished in this material force through the mental changing, or guiding, that the *spirit* may work aright.

Reading 1318-1

Q: Through my visit and in the next few months can there be a general readjustment for Mrs. [268]?

A: Within the year, not a few months. Remember, as is the experience of the entity, as is the knowledge within—such changes are a growth; they are not a shedding, for they are a growth; and require the adjustments, vibratorially, in every form and every nature.

Reading 1004-2

Q: Any other advice?

A: Each that administers, each of those that are dependent, each of the loved ones materially should know, should feel, the Divine doeth all things well. Remember that thy Pattern through suffering became the Savior. Through suffering, individuals meet themselves, and fit themselves for the Divine expression in their soul selves. The bodies that cause disturbance by the disobeying of the laws and activities in a material world are but troublesome things to the soul at times. *Life is continuous! The soul moves on*, gaining by each experience that necessary for its comprehending of its kinship and relationship to Divine.

Reading 851-1

Q: Why was my son . . . taken so early in life?

A: Seek not to find *that*, that is best to be understood in Him!

Q: Did he leave a work unfinished that I could help to carry on? If not, who could carry it on?

A: Each have their individual portion in life. As each are in, or out, or pass through these activities, there are those that are brought in line to carry on in a way as is in keeping with those forces that direct, rule or govern, that as seen.

Reading 1073-4

Q: What was the purpose of my son [988] coming into my life and passing?

A: As has been given, that each might have the opportunity for the knowing the activity one of the other.

For, as has been given, He hath not willed that any soul should perish, but with each temptation hath prepared a means, a way of escape.

Through that the individual may do for those it contacts, the soul becomes aware of those experiences of beauty, of joy. For as He hath known thee, as thou hast known thy son in the flesh, each represents, each signifies an experience that—held in the light of that given—makes for a *beauty*, a joy.

Reading 1648-2

Q: What true relation does [my departed son] bear to me, and why did he come into my life? (My third, lived five days)

A: That there might be those assurances, in spirit, in mind, in truth, of the relationship self bears to the whole.

For as the soul sought expression through the unity of activity in the material experience, this was needed in the experience of each for that assurance of love that passeth understanding, and the peace that comes with the knowledge that *His* ways are not past finding out. Though to the material mind they may oft be misunderstood, the spiritual mind bears witness as one to another.

As to the previous associations, we find these were very close—As the brother and sister, in the *Egyptian* experience.

Reading 480-37

But know that these conditions [death of child], for all, are to be used in a manner in which there is no resentment, no animosity, no blame. Just know rather that it *is*; it cannot be changed—in the present—and that the soul has preferred to stay with its Maker.

Then, the anxiety would be rather in that more and more ye *can* be, ye are—if ye take the associations in such a manner—in a closer walk with Him, who is the Giver of all good and perfect gifts; who taketh life, who giveth life; that is, in taking life it is God—and that it is withheld, it is in those conditions in which all are so overcome with disappointment, discouragement.

Do *not* blame anyone. *Do not* hold any feeling against those who may have or may not have neglected, who may not have carried out that as might have been possible; but know, thy Redeemer liveth—and that flesh of thy flesh is one again with thy Maker!

Reading 3391-1

As we find, conditions are very serious. There should not be too great a stress put upon determining to hold this body in material manifestations. Not that the hope and trust in the divine is to be lessened. Rather should it be exercised the more in realizing, even with the material, what the handicaps would be. These should give rather the parents, those so close, the feeling of their interest, of their witness before the throne of grace and mercy.

There are physical disturbances that are a part of the entity's karma. They are for lessons for those responsible for the body, if ye will accept it. If ye let it harden thee, ye miss the opportunity of knowing that He is the resurrection, He is the truth and life.

Put thy child rather at all times into the arms of Jesus.

In the physical we would apply those conditions that may aid. As developments progress, let that which is of the divine determine whether it is best in this consciousness or in the universal consciousness that it is to serve.

Reading 5678-1

In the attitudes as may be had by the body, these—as respecting mental and material *conditions—are* those things, those elements, that the body must face with that knowledge that there is an all-wise-providence, and that with the keeping in self of an ideal there is strength, comfort, understanding, that enables the body to meet the conditions which arise from day to day with the knowledge that He doeth all things well.

In that manner of mental outlook will the body find those abilities growing in self, for the steps are to be taken day by day, and sufficient unto today be that grace, that fortitude, that understanding, that will enable the mental forces to keep that balance that makes not afraid. Rather let those conditions come, then, as they may, knowing that He will give within self that knowledge of the Right to be done at the right time.

Reading 137-45

The time and the place is at hand when each may in their own way see the manifestations of the spiritual forces shown in the material world, and as each feel the weakness in their physical abilities to be of aid under the existent conditions, then doing that which seems to be as near as possible the correct condition in this time, put then the trust in Him who is the seat of Hope, Faith and of Life and of Death, and there will come through this that Peace and Joy that is beyond that that may be even conceived in the mind of him that knoweth not of that faith, for with this there will come the Peace, the Joy, and the knowing in self, "I have done my best," see? for in Him is Life and Death, and this then must be left with Him, for with this entering in by these two there may come that Peace that passeth all understanding.

Reading 1073-3

Q: Any spiritual advice?

A: Not to self alone nor to self losses give way. Rather make of life and the love thou hast felt and shown, as an *ensample*—*as* an example to others; that they may know the love thou hast to give, that is broken— yes, yet it may be mended most in *giving* same to others.

If ye would have peace, *make* peace in the lives of others. If ye would have harmony, *make* harmony or harmonious experiences in the lives of others.

The Death Experience—

Reading 993-7

Q: Am I correct in feeling that we should develop to the point where we do not have to suffer illness before dying, but should be able to keep a healthy body and just pass out of it when we have finished our work here?

A: This is an ideal, an ideal. Those who apply may attain. Those who have the price to pay, those who must meet in their application of their tenets and truths in self, must still bear their cross. That each entity must and will some day attain to the ability to be conscious of physical death without the physical suffering is true, but the day—to most—is far, too far away.

Reading 262-8

Q: At the change called death is the entity free of a physical or material body?

A: Free of the material body but not free of matter; only changed in the form as to matter; and is just as acute to the realms of consciousness as in the physical or material or carnal body, or more so.

Reading 1472-2

Q: Does death instantly end all feeling in the physical body? If not, how long can it feel?

A: This would be such a problem, dependent upon the character of which unconsciousness is produced to the physical reaction—or the manner in which the consciousness has been trained.

Death—as commonly spoken of—is only passing through God's other door. That there is continued consciousness is evidenced, ever, by the associations of influences, the abilities of entities to project or to make those impressions upon the consciousness of sensitives or the like.

As to how long—many an individual has remained in that called death for what ye call *years* without realizing it was dead! The feelings, the desires for what ye call appetites are changed, or not aware at all. The ability to communicate is that which usually disturbs or worries others.

Then, as to say how long—that depends upon the entity.

For, as has been given, the psychic forces of an entity are *constantly* active—whether the soul-entity is aware of same or not. Hence, as has been the experience of many, these become as individual as individualities or personalities are themselves.

Reading 3744-2

Q: Does the soul ever die?

A: May be banished from the Maker, not death . . .

Q: What is meant by banishment of a soul from its Maker?

A: Of the will as given in the beginning to choose for self as in the earthly plane, all insufficient matter is cast unto Saturn. To work out his own salvation as would be termed in the word, the entity or individual banishes itself, or its soul. . . .

Q: To what place or state does the subconscious pass to receive this information it gives?

A: Just here in the same sphere as when the spirit or soul or spirit and soul are driven or removed from the body or persons.

Reading 262-85

Q: Is it possible for our bodies to be rejuvenated in this incarnation?

A: Possible. For, as the body is an atomic structure, the units of energy around which there are the movements of the atomic forces that—as given—are ever the sentiment or pattern of a universe, as these atoms, as these structural forces are made to conform or to rely upon or to be one with the spiritual import, the spiritual activity, they revivify, they make for constructive forces.

How is the way shown by the Master? What is the promise in Him?

The last to be overcome is death. Death of what? The *soul* cannot die; for it is of God. The body may be revivified, rejuvenated. And it is to that end it may, the body, *transcend* the earth and its influence.

But not those standing here may reach it yet!

Reading 136-6

Q: Dreamed I died.

A: This is the manifestation of the birth of thought and mental development awakening in the individual, as mental forces and physical forces develop. This, then, is the awakening of the subconscious, as is manifested in death in physical forces; being the birth in the mental.

Reading 3744-2

Q: Is it possible for this body, Edgar Cayce, in this state, to communicate with anyone who has passed into the spirit world?

A: The spirit of all that have passed from the physical plane remain about the plane until their development carry them onward or are returned for their development here, when they are in the plane of communication or remain within this sphere, any may be communicated with. There are thousands about us here at present.

Reading 5260-1

"As the tree falls, so does it lie," saith the Maker and Giver of life. So does the light, so does the nature of an individual. For the beginnings in the next experiences are ever tempered by how sincere the purpose was of the entity in the experience before.

Reading 3817-1

Now, this is very interesting, to know that the entity known as [3817] has just come to the realization of being in the Borderland. [Died some 8 to 10 years previous to this reading.]

Reading 516-4

Q: In regard to my first projection of myself into the astral plane, about two weeks ago: Some of the people were animated and some seemed like waxen images of themselves. What made the difference?

A: Some—those that appear as images—are the expressions or shells or the body of an individual that has been left when its soul self has projected on, and has not been as yet dissolved—as it were—to the realm of that activity. For what individuals are lives on and takes form in that termed by others as the astral body. The soul leaves same, and it appears as seen. Other individuals, as experienced, are in their *animated* form through their own sphere of experience at the present.

Q: *Why did I see my father and his two brothers as young men, although I knew them when they were white-haired?*

A: They are growing, as it were, upon the eternal plane. For, as may be experienced in every entity, a death is a birth. And those that are growing then appear in their growing state.

Reading 262–92

Q: *What is meant by paradise as referred to by Jesus in speaking to the thief on the cross?*

A: The interbetween; the awareness of being in that state of transition between the material and the spiritual phases of consciousness of the Soul. The awareness that there is the companionship of entities or souls, or separate forces in those stages of the development.

Reading 967–3

He recognized all those influences in the earth that brought evil, whether manifesting as a dis-ease of body or of mind, or in the form of disease, or in jealousy, hate, malice, backbiting or all those things that are the fruits of that spirit—as death. These take many forms.

Reading 281–16

Q: *Where are the dead until Christ comes? Do they go direct to Him when they die?*

A: As visioned by the beloved, there are those of the saints making intercession always before the throne for those that are passing in and out of the interbetween; even as He, the Christ, is ever in the consciousness of those that are redeemed in Him.

Reading 262–39

Q: *What is meant by "The first shall be last and the last shall be first"?*

A: As illustrated, when life ends it begins. The end is the beginning of the transposition, or the change. The first is last, the last is first. Transposition.

Reading 5748-6

Q: *What is the significance of the empty Sarcophagi?*
A: That there will be no more death. Don't misunderstand or misinterpret! but the *interpretation* of death will be made plain.

Reading 5277-1

Q: *Is it true that "Many now living will never die," as predicted by some?*
A: No one ever dies if they believe in God. Not that those who are living materially will not die, for those who live materially, who are in a changing world, must die, and that change, that transition must come to all.

Reading 281-33

Q: *Explain the symbol of the death of the 2 witnesses.*
A: As is the symbol of—Does the individual, unless—Let's illustrate by what has been given: The Master gave, "Before the world was, I *AM*! Now if ye abide in men and I in the Father, then I will bring to thy remembrance *all things*—from the foundations of the world!"

Yet these are as dead, or the only consciousness that arises from same is that which is fanned into life or activity by the application of the laws concerning same. Hence they are as dead, yet become alive again by remembrance, by the application of thought. In what? The light of that which has been attained by the entity or soul that has applied the former lessons in its experience.

Reading 281-37

Q: *Explain what is meant by the first and second resurrections.*
A: The first is of those who have not tasted death in the sense of the dread of same. The second is of those who have *gained* the understanding that in Him there *is* no death.

Reading 295-8

Q: Did the entity repay any fraction of the debt owed the Master while He was in the earth?

A: That's impossible! For, as the entity and each soul learns, condemning self is condemning the abilities of the Master. As the Master has given, *God* is God of the *living* —*not* of the dead! For, the dead are separated from the living. As in the earth, so in the spiritual. Dead, or death, is separation. Death in the spiritual, then, is separation from life. Life, then, is God. The Master, the Christ, manifested life in the earth, through not only the material manifestations that were given in the ministry but in laying aside the life. As He gave, "I *give* my life—I give it of myself, and I take it of myself."

So, in any attempt to repay—there can be no repay! But when one lives the life that *manifests* the Christ life, love, joy, peace, harmony, grace, glory, the *joy* is in the life of the Master as He manifests—and manifested—life in the earth.

Reading 5277-1

Q: Am I right in believing the real crucifixion of Jesus consisted in the suffering He was called upon to endure in meeting the tests involved in the initiation tactics to which He was subjected before He began His ministry?

A: No. The real test was in the garden when in the realization that he had met every test and yet must know the pang of death.

Reading 3976-3

Edgar Cayce's reading volunteered (without being requested) at end of a dream interpretation reading for Mr. [900].

Have some terribly hard times in China today. In the Manchurian region, a flood and fire both. Many peoples are passing into the Borderland, their entities taking their position as has been manifest through their environment in the earth plane at present time. There are those conditions arising from this great boredom in the consciousness of many that will bring the revolution in the minds of many peoples, and begin that understanding of the purpose of the Gift of God to the World in the One made manifest in the flesh, and able to bring the consciousness made manifest in the world to the peoples. Hence many will be able through this to lay aside the physical and again manifest in a physical before men.

Reading 5749-13

In man's experience in the earth there come those periods of doubt and fear, and of the loss of hope. Then to all such there should be the reminding of that Easter Morn; and as to what it has meant and does mean in the hearts and minds of those who have and do put their trust in Jesus, the Christ.

There should be the reminding that—though He bowed under the burden of the Cross, though His blood was shed, though He entered into the tomb—through that power, that ability, that love as manifested in Himself among His fellowmen He broke the bonds of death; proclaiming in that act that *there is no death* when the individual, the soul, has and does put its trust in Him.

Thus in this hour of despair throughout the world, when those activities are such as to indicate hate, injustice, tyranny, desire to enslave or to impel others to submit to the dictates of this or that power—let all take heart and know that this, too, as the hour upon Calvary, must pass away; and that as upon the wings of the morning there comes that new hope, that new desire, to the hearts and minds of all who seek to know His face.

This must begin within thine own heart.

5

●

The Suicidal Urge

Reading 1175–1

Q: Why is suicide considered wrong? Have we the right to leave the body?

A: So long as there are those that depend upon the body! And how hath it been given? No man liveth to himself, no man dieth to himself. No man hath been so low that *some* soul hath not depended upon, relied upon same for strength.

Thus we find while there may be those experiences, these are rather of a selfish nature. But remember He gave, "Those that would offend one of these, my little ones, better that a millstone were hanged about his neck and he were cast into the depths of the sea."

Then, when thine whole body and the purposes of thine mind are to do *evil*, well that they be separated from the channel or the means of bringing offense.

Reading 2540–1

Q: Why is the thought always with me to kill myself?

A: Self-condemnation. For, not enough of that seeking to manifest God's will has been manifested. When this thought occurs, let thy prayer be as indicated:

Lord, here am I—Thine! Use me in those ways and manners as Thou seest, that I may ever glorify Thee.

57

Reading 911-7

Q: How can I desire to live more than to die, especially during two weeks or more of every month?

A: It is known by the body that this condition has been allowed to gradually increase by not doing things the body should, and by doing many things the body should not.

Then, to meet these, the *first* consideration *must* be taken in hand! The *spirit* is willing, the *flesh* is weak. *Crucify* (if necessary) the flesh and the body, but *save* the soul; save the spiritual self! and this may be accomplished through *desiring* first to *awaken* that! Hold fast to that thou knowest in self is able to *overcome* these conditions! physically acting, physically doing those things that have been outlined that are conducive to *inducing* and producing the physical effects; and that which must be met mentally in torture of body, meet it with a *smile*! knowing that it can be—it *must* be—it *will* be overcome!

Q: When I desire death more than life, how can I use my will?

A: When desire for death and the desire for life is presented, what is it that makes the life go on? The will! The spiritual life, the essence of God itself! Would the body be so weak as to crucify that it worships, rather than that which is only tagged on—in desires?

Make thy life *one with* His love! When such desires, such thoughts, even, find lodgment, look about self and see the struggle so many souls are making to keep body and soul together. How hast thou in *any* manner ministered to making *their* burden lighter?

In lightening the burden of another thine own is lightened twofold. In lightening the burdens of another the whole of will's power is strengthened many fold.

Q: How can I desire to be well, to accomplish and to fight in spite of such inner and outward conditions, difficulties—family opposition, frustrations, etc?

A: Only by the sheer will is there the desire to make beautiful the spirit of truth and life that gives animation to any desire of the body, the mind or the eye; and these conditions may *only* be met *by* that which has so oft been given: Not in self, but in the *inner* self—the God that speaks within, and in *giving* that; in thought, in act, in desire, for the welfare of others—*not of self*! Become *selfless*! and there will grow that which makes the body, the mind, *strong*—and able to meet every obstacle in the physical conditions, in the social surroundings, in the family circles, with a smile; knowing that "If my life is one with Him the rest matters *not*," and *mean* it! and *do* it! and *Be* it!

Q: What is life for and what is expected of me?

A: Use that thou hast to the glorifying *not* of self but of the Spirit that gives Life itself, that ye may *be* a companion with that source of Life that impels every thought, every desire, when not of a selfish nature.

Using that thou has for the satisfying of self's desires, self's own troubles, self's own conditions that arise, is being so self-centered as to destroy the good that may come to self.

Q: Please give me some universal truths that will best meet and help my consciousness and aid me in the material life.

A: Study in body, mind and soul to show thyself approved unto God, that gives eternal life; becoming less and less aware of the needs or *desires* that gratify the *carnal* forces in the body, and show that thou hast—by thine prayer, thine meditation—reached into the inner self sufficient to make self less and less *needful of* the material things; for what is life, that ye gain power, position, wealth, and satisfy the longings of the flesh? Are ye but to lose thine own soul by so doing? It is in thine keeping! He stands ready to help, if ye will but *let* Him help! but if self bars the door to thine consciousness, then indeed sad becomes the end!

Reading 1246-2

Q: Must I go on living?

A: Life is eternal. It is in Him, and merely to change through God's other door has only changed the outlook. But as we prepare the self for the vistas of the various consciousness upon the stages of development, we become a part of that—if our pathway is being led aright.

Reading 4415-1

. . . first there should be the study of self to that point where self has laid out that which it may do and that it may not do for its own better development in mental or physical; for in the building there is seen that each has its bounds as to that it may attain, when the building is by self alone. Well that others, as well as self, be considered—for no man . . . lives to self, no man dieth to self; for in Him is life, and the life is eternal—for the life is the gift of the Creator and is in Him, and that as builded is the application of self toward those laws as govern self in relation to that life. The life is the whole. No portion is all life, nor all life anyone portion.

Study, then, to show self approved unto the Giver of life—being not ashamed, for God—Life—is not mocked, and that the life—the body manifesting the life—sows, so shall *that* life gather of that sown, whether it be wheat, or good deeds or bad. In Him is life. Remain in Him.

Reading 1219-1

Q: *Where do I go from this planet?*

A: Where thou art preparing, and what thou art building.

Reading 69-6

Q: *What specific work did I come to this planet to do, and how much longer do I have to stay?*

A: You have to stay so long as there are the needs for the unfoldment of those that have come to rely upon the entity! Where failure has come—not failure, but rather the neglect to hold to the opportunity presented at times. How long remain in this sphere? This alone may the inner consciousness dedicate, or indicate.

Reading 4185-3

Q: *Shall I continue to live my life as heretofore, or what changes shall I make?*

A: More and more grow in grace and in the knowledge of the life's purport in this mundane sphere; for it is not all of life to live, nor yet all of death to die. Live each and every day as if the evening was to be spent with *thy* Creator, and in the *morning* of each day give thanks to the Creator for that thou may be able to give in service and self to others, that they may be blessed, even as the Creator would have them be— through thine effort. Not that self is preferred above or beyond— the other, for he that would be the greatest among men will be the servant of men. Learn what that means *in* the life, and the life will be worthwhile.

Reading 4432–1

Continue with these until they are able to reduce the amount of the narcotic or the hypnosis, or this may be *changed* to a capsule that would assist in relieving the pain or the depression, and which would be *easier* removed, though of necessity there will have to be those of common judgment used, else we will find self-destruction coming to the front in same.

Reading 5437–1

Q: Why has the patient a fear of the future? Why does he not want to live?

A: The natural tendency of the gnawing from within, and the natural pressure created in the upper portion of system from same, distorts the *view* of the body, as well as that of depressions from the associations *about* same, but with a *physical* outlook changed, the whole outlook of body—mentally *and* physically—will also be changed. Will these but be applied, we will see great *changes* in this body, mentally and physically, in three weeks. Not perfectly well, no—for then, as has been given, there should be a change in the *physical* outlook, or a change in the physical surroundings for a time.

Reading 3503–1

In giving that which as we find may be of help for this body, there must be taken into consideration the personality of the entity as well as those conditions physical, mental and material, that arise in the consciousness of the entity in the present.

There are certain ideals regarding social and moral relationships that are exercised in the mind of the entity. Ask the self: Are these changes wrought in the mind consistent with what the body has practiced in its own experience, and in the whole relationships that are a part of the present experience?

The entity should begin first with the spiritual self. What are the ideals in the spiritual self? What are the sources of thy hope for a continued consciousness after this material life? For as it may be considered, it isn't all of life just to live, nor all of death just to die, but what is prompting the hope of the future life—spiritually, mentally, materially? Are you as an individual living such a life that would be consistent in producing that ideal in relationship to all concerned in problems that are a part of the experience in the present?

Then, when the life is made consistent with the ideals, we will find health, greater relationships, greater help of every character may be experienced in the body, in the mind of this entity.

Be consistent, then, with self. Be consistent with the ideals.

Then they may be so lived in the experience as to mentally and materially demand or seek such in the relationships with others.

Do this and we will find life becoming more worthwhile—for self, for those with whom the entity comes in contact daily.

By the very living—not by word but by, deed also—make life worth living for others.

Ready for questions.

Q: *How best can I deal with an infidelity problem in my home?*

A: As ye would that others should do to you, do ye even so to them. These are problems that may be met first in self and self's ideal; then so lived that it demands the respect ye give thine own ideal.

Q: *Is there danger of a suicide from this condition?*

A: Always danger, but it's a lack of judgment. Be consistent. We are through for the present.

Reading 369-3

In the urges as are seen from the experiences in the earth's plane, we will find many of those conditions that often bother the entity in the *present* experience. Hence those injunctions that may be given here, and through the experience and urge that to develop the entity must hold ever first and foremost that of Oneness with the Creative Energy in life, in death, in the interbetween—for it is not all of life to live, nor all of death to die; for one is the birth of the other when viewed from the whole or center, and is but the experience of the entity in its transition from and to that universal center from which *all* radiation is given . . .

In the one before this we find in that land when the nomads entered into the land of Croesus and took those of that land as hostage for the tribes. The entity then the ruler's daughter, and in that school or that place so raided by the peoples, and the entity then taken as the hostage for Uhjltd, [294], the leader in this raid, and held as same by this leader until taken from him by the next in charge [195] and there remained. In the experience of the entity then in the name Elia, that horror of being forced into any action, whether of mental, physical, political, or any condition of subject to another's will. The entity lost through this experience, to the detriment of self, to the low dreg that of taking life in the way to satisfy self; not in defense of principle or of self, country or position; yet in the early portion of the life giving much to many in many ways.

Reading 5488-1

Q: What advice as to how to take up life again?

A: In the application of self to the vicissitudes of life—in the midst of life one is in the midst of death, for death is but the *beginning* of life, as life is but the beginning of an opportunity to manifest that as is *innately* built within the soul of an individual itself. To lose faith, hope, in self and in those forces which must keep for the whole of the operative forces in life, is to lose hold and to lose *confidence* in self and in self's heritage, as is given; for all are *brought* with the price, and in the application of self in *service* to another will one find that the *aptitudes* of life are but the stepping-stones to the better *understanding* of the conditions as each and every individual meets to make for them that development necessary, that they may join with those in the expressions of the divine forces as are made applicable in the lives of each and every individual. Applying self, then, in some *definite*, some individual service not as a service that is to be seen of men, but with a service eye—single to that of manifesting that faith, that hope, that expression as was given in Him, in "As oft as ye do it unto the least of these, my little ones, ye do it unto me"; for in Him is the life, and the light, and without Him there is *no* life *at all.*

Reading 3538-1

These should be thy first approach. For, as He has given, be not anxious wherewithal ye shall be clothed nor wherewithal ye shall be fed. For, the Father knoweth that ye have need of these things. When ye apply the spiritual life in thy relationships to others, there will be the supply. For, does He not clothe all nature? Are not the silver and gold

His? Then act in that manner!

Begin by reading Exodus 19:5, and know that it is meant for thee. Then read the whole of Deuteronomy 30, and know that the counsel is being given to thee, and that ye have to choose each day, now, and every other day. Don't say within self that these are of no avail to thee, but use them.

For again and again He says, "Try me—see if I will not pour out to thee a blessing."

Do that. Then as ye study, know that ye are to not only read but apply John 14, 15, 16, 17. These are not merely words, they are living truths. He came that ye might have life and have it more abundantly. He withholds no good thing from thee, if ye will only choose it, live it. Live it in thy speech to others.

Though the heavens fall, though the earth be broken up, His promises will remain—and He will not fail thee, if ye fail Him not.

6

●

Dimension of Spirit Life

Reading 816-10

Spirit is the natural, the normal condition of an entity. For hath it not been given, God is Spirit and seeketh such to worship Him, in spirit and in truth?

And then, as must be seen, must be felt, must be experienced sooner or later the awareness, the consciousness that, only *spirit* is everlasting, then the promptings, the balance must be spiritual in its essence in dealing with or judging the mental attitudes, the social relationships, the material experiences.

Reading 262-123

Q: *Give a definition of Spirit which may be given in the lesson.*

A: Spirit is the First Cause, the primary beginning, the motivative influence—as God is Spirit.

Reading 2533-1

There may be the greater expression materially of mental and spiritual aspects of each soul. While body is subject to all the influences of materiality, it may be controlled—the emotions thereof—by the mind. And the mind may be directed by spirit. Spirit is that portion of the First Cause which finds expression in all that is everlasting in the consciousness of mind *or* matter.

Reading 900–16

Q: Explain the various planes of eternity, in their order of development, or rather explain to us the steps through which the soul must pass to climb back into the arms of beloved God.

A: These, we see, must be manifest only as the finite mind in the flesh. As in the spirit forces, the development comes through the many changes, as made manifest in the evolution of man.

In the development in eternity's realm, is that a finite force as made of creation may become one with the Creator, as a unit, atom, or vibration, becomes one with the universal forces. When separated, as each were in the beginning, with the many changes possible in the material forces, the development then comes, that each spirit entity, each earth entity, the counterpart of the spirit entity, may become one with the Creator, even as the ensample to man's development through flesh, made perfect in every manner; though taking on flesh, yet without spot or blemish, never condemning, never finding fault, never bringing accusation against any, making the will one with the Father, as was in the beginning. For, without passing through each and every stage of development, there is not the correct vibration to become one with the Creator, beginning with the first vibration, as is of the spirit quickened with the flesh, and made manifest in material world (earth's plane).

Then, in the many stages of development, throughout the universal, or in the great system of the universal forces, and each stage of development made manifest through flesh, which is the testing portion of the universal vibration. In this manner then, and for this reason, all made manifest in flesh, and development, through the eons of time, space, and *called* eternity.

Q: What is this spirit entity in the body, [900], and how may he develop it in the right direction?

A: This is only the portion that develops other than in the earth's plane. Spirit entity. For soul's development is in the earth's plane. The spirit entity is in the spirit plane.

Q: Does the spirit entity have a separate consciousness apart from the physical, and is it as the consciousness of [900] when he dreams, or has visions, while asleep?

A: The spirit entity is a thing apart from any earthly connection in sleep, yet connected. For the earthly or material consciousness is ever tempered with material conditions; the superconsciousness with the consciousness between soul and spirit, and partakes of the spiritual forces principally. In consciousness we find only projections of subconscious and superconscious, which conditions project themselves in dreams, visions, unless entered into the superconscious forces. In the consciousness of earthly or material forces there enters all the attributes of the physical, fleshly body. In the subconscious there enters the attributes of soul forces, and of the conscious forces. In the superconscious there enters the subconscious forces, and spiritual discernment and development.

Reading 900-24

Q: *Have the lower forms of creation, such as animals, any life in the spirit plane?*
A: All have the spirit force.

Reading 4866-2

What it [the self] would work toward must have a great deal to do with what may be called an entirely successful operation, an entirely successful development for the body; for what the body sets as its ideal, whether that which is wholly of the material or that which is a well balanced spiritual, mental and material condition, will be those developments; for the activity—whether of wholly material conditions, mental conditions, or of spiritual conditions—is the *spirit* with which an entity, a body, goes about its activity. If the life is to become wholly mechanical, or wholly material minded, then only the material will be the natural result, and this will *not* bring contentment—nor will it satisfy. If the ideal will be set as a well-balanced self, knowing that the spirit, the life—that is, the spirit *is* the life, the mental attitude is the development or the builder—then the results will be in that comparison as to the activity that is given in respect to these attitudes.

Reading 4595-1

The sympathetic forces [are] the seat of all of the soul and spirit forces [in the physical body].

Editor's Note: The sympathetic nervous system includes the seven endocrine glands, which other Cayce readings identify as the physical portions of the seven chakras.

Reading 3744–2

Q: Please give a definition of psychic phenomena.

A: *Psychic* means of the *Spirit* or *Soul*, for cooperation of the Phenomena, or manifestation of the workings of those forces within the individual, or through the individual, from whom such phenomena, or of such phases of the working of the spirit and soul, to bring the actions of these to the physical plane, Phenomena meaning only the act itself, brought to the attention, or manifested in such a way as to bring the attention of an individual to the work itself.

Psychic in the broader sense meaning spirit, soul, or the imagination of the mind, when attuned to the various phases of either of these two portions of the entity of an individual, or from the entity of others who are passed into the other planes than the physical or material; yet in the broader sense, the Phenomena of Psychic forces is as material as the forces that become visible to the material or physical plane.

Psychic forces cover many various conditions, depending upon the development of the individual, or how far distant the entity is from the plane of spirit and soul forces.

Psychic means not understood from the physical, or material, or conscious mind.

Psychic means that of the mind presenting the soul and the spirit entity as manifested in the individual mind. Then taking the phases of that force, we find all Psychic Phenomena or force, presented through one of the acknowledged five senses of the physical or material body—these being used as the mode of manifesting to individuals. Hence we would have in the truest sense, *psychic*, meaning the expression to the material world of the latent, or hidden sense of the soul and spirit forces, whether manifested from behind, or in and through the material plane.

Editor's Note: Cayce saw a distinction between our soul and our spirit, as indicated in this next reading.

Reading 900-17

Q: It has been given that the soul is the spiritual force that animates or gives life to the body. What is spirit? What is spiritual force? Is it corporeal or incorporeal? Where may we find the soul force in the body—in the brain, nerve centers or where?

A: There is a vast deal of difference between spiritual and soul forces, for, as given, each force there has been set guards or bounds. Spirit forces are the animation of *all life* giving life–producing forces in animate or inanimate forces. Spiritual elements become corporeal when we speak of the spiritual body in a spiritual entity; then composed of spirit, soul and the superconsciousness.

In the soul forces, and its dwelling in man, we find the animation, the spiritual element, the soul that developing element, and contained in the brain, in the nerve, in the centers of the whole system. As to the specific centers, nearer those centers of the sensory system, physically speaking.

In the conditions, then, we find when soul and spirit take flight from the animate forces of an human, we find the deadening of all the centers of the sensory system, with the vitality of the solar plexus system, with the gland of the medulla oblongata, these then controlling the forces, and the life becomes extinct, with soul and spirit, with the superconscious forces, gone.

Then, we have as this:

Spiritual element, the vitality, produces the motive forces of the entity, whether physical or spiritual. Spiritual forces being the life, the reproductive principle; the soul the development principle. As we have manifested, or illustrated, in the physical body in nerve tissue: There becomes that principle of the nerve action and the nerve in action. That is, with the expression of some condition bringing distress in the body, the active principle is the spirit. The nerve is the soul, for development.

Q: What happens to the conscious mind forces and physical forces at death?

A: The conscious mind forces either are in the soul's development, and in the superconsciousness, or left with that portion of material forces which goes to the reclaiming, or remoulding, of physical bodies, for indwelling of spiritual entities.

Reading 257–238

Q: Did I conduct myself properly with the people I have met so far at the War Department?

A: We do not find fault, but this of course should be determined by self—rather than from other sources. Remember, these conditions exist, and keep this ever before thee: The real intent and purpose in declarations call from the spiritual forces that influence which is for good or bad. That, to be sure, is free will. Hence the injunctions as have been so oft given the body—do not appear to be that ye really are not. Be sincere with self and ye will not be false or insincere with others. The spirit of truth brings the outward appearance of that desire first suggested, if the body and mind are in keeping with that as would be pleasing to the influences or forces called God. For, the declaration of each soul sets in motion that spirit. What spirit do ye entertain? Truth, justice, mercy, love, patience, brotherly kindness? Or self, self-praise, self-glory that ye may be wellspoken of materially? These choices are made by the individual. Their results, their effects in the lives of individuals are such as to determine spiritual success, material success, or a well-rounded mental, spiritual *and* material success. For, the earth is the Lord's and the fulness thereof. The abilities that have been lent thee, keep inviolate—if ye would be in keeping with His purposes with thee.

Thou hast the ability to bring truth and light to many. These are then within thine own keeping, according to the manner in which ye conduct thyself before others. With what spirit, with what purpose do ye serve?

Reading 816–3

Much of that the entity has thought, has experienced, is cherished more from within. Yet, if there were some changes in these directions, there may be a greater joy in the living in this experience. For while that sojourn gives those influences which make for abilities in being able to cope with conditions and experiences in the lives of individuals and groups and masses, if these are held only in self and not given out with that love of service, for the abilities within self to give expressions of the love of a divine Father, they may become stumblingblocks in thine experience. For all force, all manifestations in materiality are the expressions of spirit, and are *prompted* by same. Are these influences of the divine, or dost thou cherish those that at times may become questioned? Know in what, in whom, thou hast believed, and know whether it be of a constructive or of a growing influence for the spirit of truth or not. For the promise is given to all, "My spirit beareth witness with thy spirit as to whether thou art choosing good or evil in all of thy ways."

Reading 1257–1

Know that the *living* forces of thy God are *active!* Not as of stone or wood but as the spirit of truth that casteth out fear, that bringeth peace, that bringeth harmony, that bringeth those things that make for the associations with thy fellow man as a better neighbor, a better sister, a better daughter, a better mother, a better citizen.

Reading 1265–1

What, then, *is* thine ideal? Is it founded in that ye yourself may do, or that in which ye may be the *channel* through which others may find *their* association with a *living* God, a living ideal, a living love, a living faith, a living experience of joy? *These* be they which are of the truth, and thus grow as does the spirit of truth.

7

●

Spirit Is the Real Life

Reading 1998–1
But know, all has its concept in spirit—then mind; and mind is the builder.

Reading 1999–1
For remember, *mind* is the builder between the things spiritual (from which all emanate) and that which is material (which is the manifestation that mind seeks to bring ever into the experience of all).

Reading 2062–1
Hence again the injunction—look upon all phases; for there is the mental, the material and the spiritual, and these are the phases of man's reaction and man's activity. Do not apply the law of the spiritual in material things, nor the material in spiritual things. Remember that mind is the builder, and the spirit giveth life. And as ye use and dwell upon such, be sure thy ideal is in Him.

Reading 2247–1
But keep the spiritual life first. The mental and material should be the outgrowth, the result of spiritual attainments.

Reading 2281-1

Depart not from the faith thou findest in Him, and may it be renewed as the spirit ever is within thee. For the spirit is the life. The life is the purpose, the desire. Make them sure in Him.

Reading 2322-2

Know that all must first be conceived from the spiritual, and then magnified or grown through the mental application as an experience coming into material application in the lives of others.

Q: Can suggestions be made as to how self mastery can be developed; that is, will power and initiative?

A: Study that from the spiritual angle, if there would be that power, that might to succeed. For, as has been given, all first finds concept in the spiritual. The mental is the builder. This is true in planning the life, the relationships, and every phase of man's existence or experience.

Reading 2328-1

First, know thine own ideals—physical, mental, spiritual. Know that the spiritual and mental, and the material, must arise from that which is of spiritual concept; for only the spirit *and* mental are eternal, and only that of the mental that is spiritual in its concept—or creative in its relationships to things, conditions, experiences, places or individuals.

Reading 2357-1

Yes, we have the body and those conditions as surround same, [2357]. Now, we find there are those conditions as are abnormal for this body, and these may, in the correct application of those conditions and elements necessary, be brought to a much better and a nearer normal functioning of this body. While conditions are aggravated at times, and while seemingly there is little that may be accomplished in the physical to correct some of the conditions that disturb the body, there should first be gained the consciousness by this body that there are those elements in the physical condition of each body that will bring that for the physical functioning of that body that necessary conditions for the body to meet the needs of the body, in the physical, then mental, the moral, and the spiritual welfare of the conditions. Spirit is life, whether related to the physical functioning of the atomic forces within the system or whether that of the mental being of a body, and these must coordinate in the proper direction one with another, just as much as it is necessary for a physical functioning organ to coordinate with the rest of the system. For instance, here, with this body, there have been times when seemingly little or nothing would be assimilated or digested by the body. The necessity of assimilation is as much necessary as the desire for food; for what profit it a body to desire to eat, will the food eaten not assimilate and build that necessary for the sustenance and replenishing of the physical body? There is seen in the physical forces that there has existed, and does exist, certain disturbances in the nervous system. These have to do with both the cerebro-spinal and sympathetic nerve system. In the physical functioning of a body, the subligations or impingements of nerve or nerve plexuses, or nerve branches, become a *physical* action, and these in their turn produced, or produce, physical results; while conditions or disturbances in plexus that control, or are controlled by certain reflexes from the cerebro-spinal to the sympathetic system, may not so easily be directed by the removal of pressure in a portion of the body. What is active upon such conditions, then, that these may be aided? That of the *physical* is the vibratory rate at which the nerve functions to produce coordination in the functioning of the system, as related to the *sensory* organism or as is seen with this body, there are disturbances in the functioning of *organs* of the sensory system. These organs possess, and have, their individual machine apparatus for the functioning of the system in the direction in which that organism or organ is to function, or its own modus operandi is within itself a portion of the whole, yet dependent upon the coordination of both the cerebro-spinal and sympathetic to function in its proper relation with that organ of the system, that that as is assimilated, that as is builded in the system, may produce that *necessary* for the proper vibratory forces as to bring the result of the condition desired, or, as in this case, in the hearing, or as in the feeling. The auditory forces, then, abnormal to the conditions as should be created in this body here . . .

Reading 2390-1

Numbers, too, become at times an influence; as three and its multiples being the phases of the entity in its various moods, or in its various manners of seeking. For, the entity finds—within itself—there *is* the physical, with all its emotions; the mental with its abilities to grasp and to build and to *change* the aspects of the physical if they be purely of the bodily forces or those conditions or thoughts or individual experiences; as well as the spiritual from which emanates the essence of all power, might and strength! Rely upon that more.

Reading 2408-1

In material manifestation, or the activities of these principles in a causation or three-dimensional world, one gradually realizes then the less of self and the more of world, one gradually realizes then the less of self and the more of the creative forces in the experience; thus bringing one closer to the understanding that like begets like—that what is sown in spirit may *grow* in mind, may find fruit in materiality—and that this changed may be just the reverse—that the dwelling upon material influence of selfish natures separates spirit from the control of mind, the builder.

Reading 2533-6

That is as the spirit. And as the spirit builds, as the spirit forms in its activity in mind, the mind becomes then the builder. The mind is not the spirit, it is a companion to the spirit; it builds a pattern. And this is the beginning of how self may raise that expectancy of its period of activity in the earth. And this is the beginning of thy ideal. Of what? Of that the soul should, does, will, can, must, accomplish in this experience!

Reading 2647-1

This is lack of self-confidence. This is lack of the *ideal* that is spiritual. For, know, all things material have first their inception in the spiritual. Then they give or take form in the mental, finding expression in the material. Illustrate this in that as brings to mind the concept of the music of nature, the music of the spheres, the music of the birds, the poetic expressions that oft rise to thy mind. These gradually give impressions.

Reading 2709-1

One of noble purposes, and given to good works towards others, especially that as relates to building of the mental abilities of an individual. In this respect there may be given that to the entity here, which—correlated with those ideas as have been and are being building within self towards self's development—would be well to apply in this present experience; that is, the life of every atomic force is the *spirit* of same. The mental is the builder, and the physical or sensuous manifestation is the result—and that life projects itself in that manner in which it is directed by that builded in the continuity of the life force as is radiated through that builded. See?

Reading 2727-1

First, as to thy ideal of moral and mental relationships—know that these are altogether founded in spiritual aspects. For, as the body finds itself—it is body, mind, soul. The soul lives on, builded by the mind. The body is the material manifestation. Know thy ideal.

Reading 2747-1

First, find self—and know thy own ideal, spiritually, mentally, materially. And know that the material fadeth away, the mental may bring life or death according to the choice of the mind itself.

Then in mind and in body the entity must have its life in spirit. For, this alone abideth forever.

Reading 2751-1

Q: How may I help my daughter, [. . .], to solve her marital problem?

A: These can best be studied in the light of those suggestions indicated as to the application of self through the various experiences in the earth.

Remember, if the spiritual is put first and foremost, if the purpose of an individual is in the *right* direction, the *material* happenings will eventually come right. These may at times appear confusing and as being contradictory, but the law of the Lord is *perfect*.

To enable an individual to find these is the understanding where *all* marital relationships may be best understood.

Individuals do not meet by chance. They *are* necessary in the experiences of others, though they may not always use their opportunities in a spiritual way or manner.

Thus the injunction—study to show thyself approved unto thy ideal, which *is* thy God. If ye make thyself god, if ye make thy hopes, thy wants, thy purposes thy god, they become selfish, they become monsters, they become destroying influences.

Teach, give instruction, even as ye did in the Egyptian experience. There ye aided. Now ye may aid; not by material.

And *do not* condemn anyone!

Reading 2772-1

For, life is God, or eternity, and thus is a continuous thing. Various consciousnesses in various spheres of activity are only as a part of the experience, as the mind is the controlling and the building force in the physical being. For, Mind is the Builder. That which is of the spirit is that which is proposed, while that in the physical is as the result of material application.

Reading 2776-1

Find thy ideal, spiritually, mentally and materially. Know that all force has its expression first in spirit. True, mind is the control—through that activity comes the material expression of same.

Reading 2786-1

These may become stumblingblocks in the entity's experience even in the present. Look to that which is an ideal, and be sure it is founded in that of spiritual import. For, every fact has its inception in spirit; mind is the builder, the material expression is the outcome of one of these upon the other. The spirit is of creation, or God; the mind is as of an individual taking hold upon both materiality and spirituality. The choice is in the hands of the individual. Use thy talents well.

Reading 2787-1

We find in Jupiter the universal consciousness. Notice its position, though, in thy awareness. Move it toward the front, rather than toward the end. For, first in spirit, then in mind, then is the materialization. For, mind is the builder; even as ye find thy body, thy mind, thy soul the three-dimensional experience of an individual that become comparable with the Father, the Son and the Holy Spirit. The Son is the Mind. He *is* the way. So the mind of self is the way.

Reading 2788-1

The entity seeks to know first causes. Remember, these arise from spiritual concepts. For, it is first in spirit, then in mind, then the material manifestation; whether this is association with individuals or things, or whether it has to do with universal activity as in the nature of things. For, it is the purpose with which individual man makes application to the things about him, that brings about the physical or material result. "With what spirit, with what purpose, do ye these things?"

Reading 2801-1

Now, in the physical, mental and spiritual forces in this body, which complete the entity at this time, we have a good manifestation of the entity in a psychological understanding and manifestation of the psychology of an entity, for we find the mental rules in this entity, as it should in the earth plane, and the physical is under subjugation of the mental proclivities of the entity. That is, we have in this entity one well rounded to a completion of the forces in the earth plane, for there is much spiritual understanding with the mental forces, and the entity needs only to keep all the forces well rounded in that straight and narrow way that leads to the perfect understanding.

As to the physical conditions, we find in the present forces these are very good in many respects. There are some conditions that the body needs from the physical, from the mental, from the spiritual aspect, to be wary of, for the soul, spirit and the physical must ever remember the physical body, the material body, is but the temple through which the mental forces, with the will, builds to that I AM that must ever live, and without the perfect balanced forces the best cannot be given or manifested through the present entity's forces.

Reading 2813–1

First, know thy ideals—physical, mental and spiritual. And know the physical result is first conceived in spirit, acted upon by mind, and then manifested in the material—with what spirit ye entertain.

Reading 2900–2

Know thy ideal spiritually, the application of same mentally, and ye will find the material things will come in their own way and time.

For, in the material world the spiritual concept is the basis of the trend, or of the mind; and from same arises the material results. When such relationship, or when any relationship is altered otherwise, it may become a stumblingstone rather than a steppingstone for unfoldment.

Reading 2995–3

Know, then, that these also apply to the entity concerning same: The body, mind and soul of the entity are one. They are represented here as a physical body—very good in many respects. A very analytical mind, but as indicated, one who tends to draw judgements rather severely. Know that there are laws pertaining to such in mind as well as in spiritual and in material. For whatever there may be is first conceived in spirit. It is acted upon by mind. Dependent, then, upon what the mind of the entity holds as its ideal, or as to what form or manner it would give give by and through what spirit it would build in its mental self.

Reading 3053–3

Many stress spirituality when the mind is used as the measuring stick. Many stress physical manifestation when mind is used as the measuring stick. Many interpret spiritual things and attempt to use physical activity as the measuring stick. Many attempt to interpret spiritual things, using the mind as the measuring stick. But each phase of thine own experience should be interpreted in its proper sphere of activity, so that when ye interpret thy music, thy love, thy friendships, thy associations, thy activities with others, it will be in the proper sphere according to thy whole purpose in the earth—to glorify thy Maker; if there would be the full interpretation of "The Lord thy God is one" and "Thou shalt love thy brother as thyself." O that men would find, there is nothing mentioned here about the physical or the mind, but the spiritual attitude one takes in self respecting such!

Reading 3064-1

When the Appliance is used, do use the period for meditation upon *spiritual* things; knowing that all healing, all correcting of the spiritual and of the mental life must come from the divine within, and the results in the physical being will be in keeping with that which is developed in the spiritual self.

Reading 3083-1

Yet, learn the lesson: that physical must be met in the physical, that mental must be met in the mental, and that spiritual is the directing force—but Mind is the Builder.

Reading 3132-1

The material is of the earth-earthy. The spiritual is of the heavenly or the motivative forces. The mental is ever the builder.

That as would be manifested must first be in spirit, then in mind, then in material activity. For, this is the evolution of the earth, the evolution of things, the evolution of ideas and of ideals. For, He came into the earth that through Him man might have access again to the grace and mercy of those spiritual forces that are the directing ideals of each soul-entity.

Reading 3184-1

Then, these are the things the entity should analyze the more in self—as will be seen from the periods of expression in the earth—as to what are the promptings of the individual's urges. For each individual finds the motivative influence of its life within its own self, and that is correct—as was stated of old by the lawgiver; Think not as to who will descend from heaven to give a message or who would come from over the sea that ye might learn and understand. For lo it is within thine own heart, thine own mind. Thy body is indeed the temple of the living God. He has promised to meet thee and, know that all in the mental, all in the material, has its inception, it conception, in spirit, in purpose, in

hope, in desire. Know thy relationship, then, first, with that ye hope for.
For life (or God), immortality of the soul, is real; as may be seen from
thine own urges—if ye analyze them correctly.

Reading 3190-2

Q: In what way can the body control the physical through the mental?

A: The mental ever controls the physical, when guided in those chan-
nels that gives the awakening in the physical of the Divine in self. In
that channel may the body guide the physical through the mental, for
ever will we find that the "spirit beareth witness with My Spirit," as to
the control to make the mental, the physical, the spiritual in the body
One with *that force* giving the life in the body.

Reading 3198-3

What is manifested in the material affairs or activities of the entity is
first perceived or conceived in the spiritual imports of the entity. These
are cultivated or entertained in the mental and thus physical results are
evidenced.

Reading 3241-1

Q: What spiritual qualities should be stressed?

A: Know that all that is in material manifestation is first of spirit; then
by mind (the builder) is brought into realization. Then by the power of
the might that is in Him and in His promise, keep that faith which has
been indicated for the entity.

Reading 3308-1

Thus in the dedicating of thy mind, of thy body, may the soul express—through the activities of mind and body—that which is in keeping with that the Master gave—"If ye love Me, keep My commandments,
and I—and the Father—will come and abide with thee." These are not
merely symbols, signs or tenets, but may be made practical in the lives
of individuals that ye may instruct day by day; not by any set form. For,
if the Lord is one, He is in the storm as in the stillness, in the stars as in
the sand in *activity*. For life itself is the manifestation of the oneness of
the Father manifested in the Son, who came to give life and it—life more

abundantly. For, He is the life, the resurrection, the way. These ye should teach, these ye should practice in thy conversation, in thy daily dealings with thy fellow man.

Reading 3333-1

Q: How can I know I am in the right work and be contented with it?

A: "My spirit beareth witness with thy spirit." Not only is this applicable in spirit but in mind and in body. For, know, the Lord is one. All that becomes active in the mind is first in spirit. Then in mind does it grow. Then it materiality does it take shape.

Reading 3350-1

Thus innately the entity is ever desiring to try something new. This is well, provided the basis of such is builded upon truth. For truth in any clime is ever the same—it is law. And love is law, law is love. Love is God, God is Love. It is the universal consciousness, the desire for harmonious expressions for the good of all, that is the heritage in man, if there is the acceptance of the way and manner such may be applied, first in the spiritual purpose and then in the mental application, and the material success will be pleasing to any.

Reading 3351-1

Know that of such, yea of people, would be known that faults and successes do not come from thought. Thought is the builder, but spirit is the motivating force. What spirit do you entertain? If it be of God, it can not fail, if it be of self or the devil a failure may be in the offing, dependent upon the measure with which ye mete same—as through the experience of the entity as Marcelle Ney.

Reading 3359-1

Find that, and ye will begin then with the correct attitude. For, that we find in spirit taketh form in mind. Mind becomes the builder. The physical body is the result.

Reading 3376-2

But what is thy yardstick of ideals? All that is material once existed in spirit, or the soul of the entity. Mind becomes the builder, the physical becomes the result. It depends, then, upon the materials—or the spirit with which one is prompted.

Reading 3394-2

In Jupiter an ennobling influence has made the entity ever mindful of the need of a universal consciousness towards the follow man, even for material gains in the earth. There needs to be a warning that there be the more application for the spiritual needs, the spirit of the law of love and of friendship, rather than the letter of the law. For those who would have friends or who would succeed materially must begin with the spirit that is entertained. If the spirit is for self or is of a selfish nature, or one of spite or greed, it must eventually turn upon thee.

Reading 3424-1

Also in Jupiter we find the interest in morality, religion, good living, personality. These shall all be approached, to be sure, from individuality; and the basis of the individuality of an entity must come from its ideal spiritually. For all is born first in spirit, then in mind, then it may become manifested in the material plane. For God moved and the heavens and the earth came into being. God is spirit. Man with his soul, that may be a companion to the Creative Forces, is of that same source. Thus to grow in grace and knowledge, one applies, one has, one uses one's spiritual self. And with what spirit we apply, we grow also in mind and in body.

Reading 3463-1

Astrologically we find urges from Mercury, Saturn, Mars, Uranus. These bring the high mental abilities. In Saturn there is ofttimes not the consideration of others nor the sources from which all good must arise. For it can only come from one source, and it is not material alone. The material is merely the result. It must be builded in spiritual purposes. It must be builded according to the spirit with which a soul-entity is entertained or moved.

Reading 3481-1

Individuals can become too zealous or too active without consideration of the physical, mental and spiritual. True, all influences are first spiritual; but the mind is the builder and the body is the result. Spiritualizing the body without the mind being wholly spiritualized may bring such results as we find indicated here, so as to raise even the kundaline forces in the body without their giving full expression.

Reading 3513-1

For that which occurs in physical or in mind is first prompted in spirit, and thus are the activities of the entity correlated one to another, not only in this experience but throughout the consciousness of the entity in the various spheres or varied periods of material activity with a physical consciousness.

Reading 3541-1

But first we would give these: Know that all that comes into materialization or into physical being is first patterned in mind and in spirit. Mind is the builder, and your purpose is dependent upon what spirit—or what mortar, what water—those things that go to make materiality active in the earth—you use, as to what is the character of the body mind or structure that ye, as an entity, create.

Reading 3582-2

For as the entity realizes, there is little or nothing that happens by chance, but ever after a pattern, a law. And that the entity may build in the mind from the spiritual, that it accepts as its director alters results that may be had in the experience of the individual—in the same measure as was asked "Master, who sinned—this man or his parents, that he was born blind?"

Reading 3590-2

The spiritual self is life, the activity of the mental and of the physical is of the soul—and thus a soul-body.

Reading 3611-1

The entity must learn that this must be as much in the mental, or more. For the physical is the result of the spiritual ideals, and the mind as the builder brings those results. True, the body must at times have its discipline, but this is rather of mind and spirit as well as physical discipline.

Reading 3639-1

Then, the entity should become well founded in relationship with Creative Forces. For any activity begins first in spirit, then in mind, and then in the material world. And mind is the builder. It is that which builds for whatever may be the contributing factor from the abilities of individuals, as well as self's application in same.

Reading 3704-1

Q: What is the purpose of this life on earth for me?

A: As indicated, in applying self in greater welfare activities for others, and in the preparation of and in building the home. First it must be spiritual, then it must be mental and then it may be in the physical.

Reading 3902-2

As urges latent and manifested, many are the manifestations in the consciousness and in the urges of the entity indicating unusual abilities to manifest in a material world. From the urges, from sojourns during the interims we find Mercury, Mars, Venus, Jupiter. No better array might be set, and yet—as in spirit, so in mind—these must be attuned, used, applied. For though there may be purpose, ability, strength, without being used it is nil and of none effect.

Reading 3975-1

Yes, we have the body here. We find there are abnormal conditions in this body, [3975] we are speaking of. These have more to do with specific causes in the physical. Keep in touch with this here if you would get this. The conditions as we have given here have more to do in the physical body than we have to do with that between the spirit and soul or mental force in the body here for there are in the physical body the material change or difference that must be brought about to make the whole body work in accord and create a perfect equilibrium through-out the whole system in this body. If we would correct the condition so that the whole life giving force or fluids in the body have their course in their proper accord throughout the system and could give to all the portions of this body the life giving forces then we will find that the rejuvenation of all forces of the body will be brought to normal and that we have the physical forces with the mental and divine forces all carried out throughout their whole forces in the body and bring the mental and spirit forces to a development to better understanding of itself. The physical force in this system has been brought into this body that it may learn and develop more through the mental and spiritual forces that it is to carry on with these from time to time. This it must understand in self.

Reading 4035–1

We find in Mars the very decided points or ideas or stands that the entity may take on subjects; but as warned concerning the experience before this as a critic, if you criticize then you may expect to be criti-cized yourself. For the law of the Lord is perfect and it is as applicable in man as in the universe, as in nature, as in the realms of spirit itself. For the first principle is that the Lord, the God of the universe is one. What is effective or active in spirit (where it forms first) must be active and must influence the imaginative influences of an individual entity. For the entity finds itself a body, a mind, a soul—three; or the earth con-sciousness as a three–dimensional plane in one.

Reading 4041–1

Know these as facts: That which is manifested physically or mentally has its concept or urge arising from the spiritual aspects of the entity, or the spirit, the purpose, the sources, the urges entertained by the entity. If such purposes and ideals or urges are of and through creative forces, then the mental (as the builder) may become constructive or creative. Then the physical or final manifestation will be good. That the changes may come doesn't necessarily indicate that the spiritual urge is in error but that the manner or way of application in the mental may be in the wrong direction.

Reading 4143-1

In the mental we find those abilities to mete out much that may be helpful to others in their understanding their relationships with their fellow man, as well as their relationship with the spiritual influences that may be manifest in the material plane. Materially, we find spiritual forces are the life, the background, the basis for all activity; the mental is the builder; the physical is the result that accrues from such activity in the material or in the carnal plane.

Reading 4405-1

In the physical forces, keep fit—keep the *mental* attuned properly, and the *spiritual* life *will* guide in all things! Oft is it considered by individuals that the spiritual life and mental life are things apart. They *must* be one—they *are* one, even though individuals attempt to separate. The *spirit* is the life, the motive force, that behind all life itself, and the mind-physical and the mind of the soul—or that spirit force itself—is guiding, directing—not always guarding, but may be trained in that direction. Hence, seek that of the spiritual within self *first*, and *all these* things of *earthly* nature will be *added* in their proper place, their proper association, their proper connections.

Reading 4609-1

In the urge in conditions existent in the present physical relations with the universal forces, we may find much with this entity worthy of study by those who hold to tenets respecting continuity of life and its relation with the varied appearances of an entity through the experiences in the earth's plane; for to the physiognomist there is presented that, in the mental and physical being of the entity or body present, which would be proof positive of that law given as concerning how that life manifested in the earth plane is first the life spiritual, the life mental, the physical a result of that builded and coming in manifested form irrespective of that that has been often misapplied or misdirected towards environmental or hereditary conditions; for we find the lives of those whom this entity's being in the present plane manifested through were in accord with that same law, and brought into being that which—through the existent conditions of environmental nature—presented the channel for that manifested life as builded by the individual entity, and the entity sought that channel for its manifestation in the earth's plane at that stage of its development, or—as man would physically call it—at that time.

Reading 4722-1

Q: Any spiritual advice for the body?

A: Awaken that within self to the abilities, to the qualities that the body may experience through the activity of the spiritual forces within self, that will give the reactions and make the effects as may be created in the physical; for the spiritual is the life, the mental is the builder, and the physical or material is the result.

Reading 4866-2

As has been outlined, this also must be taken into consideration, as the body seeks for those developments in self from the mental and material conditions in the affairs of self—that as self sets as its ideal. What it would work toward must have a great deal to do with what may be called an entirely successful operation, an entirely successful development for the body; for what the body sets as its ideal, whether that which is wholly of the material or that which is a well balanced spiritual, mental and material condition, will be those developments; for the activity—whether of wholly material conditions, mental conditions, or of spiritual conditions—is the *spirit* with which an entity, a body, goes about its activity. If the life is to become wholly mechanical, or wholly material minded, then only the material will be the natural result, and this will *not* bring contentment—nor will it satisfy. If the ideal will be set as a well balanced self, knowing that the spirit, the life—that is, the spirit *is* the life, the mental attitude is the development or the builder, then the results will be in that comparison as to the activity that is given in respect to these attitudes.

Reading 5001-1

These are problems you are meeting in self in the present. For ye had the same companion through that experience. Thus let that of duty from the spiritual self be the guiding influence. For the entity finds self with a body which it can get along with very well! It can use its own judgments, its own appetites, its own activities. The mind becomes something else! and these influences should be governed by spiritual import, spiritual purpose. Know that what is first conceived is in spirit. In mind does it grow to an activity which becomes either creative or self-satisfying, self-gratifying.

Reading 5118–1

Before this the entity was in the land of the present sojourn. Hence those attractions that have brought the entity to the present environs. For the entity is a "sensitive", as indicated in the manner in which it studies the anatomical structure, as well as the mind structure. Not enough stress is put on the spiritual, for the sources. For, what comes in mind, in materiality, must first have been created in the spirit. For the earth was first without form and void. So is mind, or matter. It is first a desire, a consciousness, a fluid, a gas. It is united, it becomes, as it were, as a "feeling" for. So may the entity in itself find the same. These are of particular interest to the entity.

Reading 5502–3

Q: What can [257] further do in his daily life to show himself more approved unto the Giver of these gifts?

A: Study to show thyself approved unto God, avoiding the appearances of evil, knowing that as the acts of thine going-ins and coming-outs [are] that reflection of the God ye would serve. If that God be money, power, position, fame, these must reflect in the lives and the life of the acts of self. Will those forces as were made manifest as of old when Abraham [was] called to go out to make a peculiar people, a different nation, so again may the body hear that called as when offering in the temple that "Mine people have wandered astray", yet in the little here, the word there, the precept and example, may they again know Jehovah in His Holy Place.

Necessary that each individual have their own problems given that attention as seemeth to them necessary, but as and when ones [are] well-grounded in the truths of the universe that may know through that given them that the spirit is life, the spirit of service is strength, and [that it] aids in every condition in man's experience.

Reading 5534-1

Q: What will his attitude be when he returns?

A: In answer to that as is desired in self; for desire is of a threefold nature, and that builded in self finds its response in another, and as there is the *sincere* desire to build in the mental being of any in which such relationships have existed, as in this condition, that will be builded—for life, in all its phases, is of the threefold nature. *Spirit* is willing; *mind* is the builder; the *result* is that *manifested* in the material conditions as surround a body. That attitude, then, will be that as has been builded, as has been desired in self as related to another.

Reading 5642-3

We have the body here—we have had this before, you see. Now we find there are improvements in the physical forces of this body since last we had same here. There are many conditions to be considered respecting those conditions that exist in the physical being of the body, and while there arise from time to time those elements that are of a disturbing and discouraging nature to the body, these [the epilepsy attacks] will of necessity have to be by the body put in the background and not allow these conditions—because they do occur occasionally—to gain control over the mental body; for while physical conditions are reacting to the mental being, the mental body *is* the builder. The physical is the result, and the spiritual will build that as is builded in the mental being, and a physical result is then amenable to outside influences that are mental, material, and physical. Hence there are being applied in the physical being of this body those conditions that, while these are material—and while the mental body is in the condition of being disturbed, this gives rise to those conditions of discouragement. This must have the outside influence to give the proper incentive in a correlated effect or correlated manner to this body, so that the whole physical reaction will be in keeping with that as the mental being would have the body be. Then, be consistent—persistent—in the spiritual, mental and physical application of all those conditions that apply to the physical body, to the material body, to the mental body, and the *spiritual* will guide and lead aright. For we are one in Him, and ourselves may only get in the way of a full development. Then keep those, as yet, as have been given, and be patient in well-doing. Do not be overcome, but overcome evil with good. Materially, mentally, physically, apply this in the body. Do that.

Reading 5642–4

Keep the inhalant; also keep the manipulations as often as is *convenient* for the body to do so. Keep in the open. Do not overtax the mind, but keep sufficient physical exercise to keep proper coordination, and we will find the near normal conditions will yet come to this body. Keep the mental in attunement to the spiritual side of life, and remember that the spiritual will build that, that the *mental* will attune itself for a physical or materialization in the flesh; for the spiritual forces are the same one day after another, and unto the end.

Reading 5680–1

In the spiritual development of self: These are as the greater forces that come to everyone, for, as is seen, while the body physical presents as a unit a oneness, yet same is made up of the spiritual, the mental and the physical. The spiritual the creator, the mental the builder, the material—that of the result of a life, a thought, a deed; for thoughts are deeds and may be miracles or crimes in their execution and the end thereof.

Reading 5735–1

That, Life is in that way of continuity; and Life is *all*; and no one portion of Life is the whole; for Life is that given of the *spirit*; and the Soul is as the individual. The mental—whether that of a sensuous consciousness or of the super, or the objective consciousness—is the Builder; and that *builded*, whether in the physical or soul body, is the Result.

8

●

Life Beyond Earth

Editor's Note: As much as we identify with planet Earth and our terrestrial life here, Edgar Cayce's reading of the Akashic Records and the Universal Consciousness tells a different story. From Cayce's perspective, we were, are, and will be again *celestial* beings, traversing the vast expanse of space. Our primal mission is to know ourselves and our Creator. Cayce often began readings for individuals by identifying their planetary and stellar influences, explaining that these were influences because of the soul's journeys through those dimensions. Before and after incarnating into this world and physical life, the soul experiences dimensions beyond the earth plane.

I've edited the following reading for clarity and focus on the topic:

Reading 311-2

As an entity passes on from this present time or this solar system, this sun, these forces, it passes through the various spheres—on and on through the *eons* of time or space—leading first into that central force known as Arcturus—nearer the Pleiades. Eventually, an entity passes into the inner forces, inner sense, then they may again—after a period of nearly ten thousand years—enter into the earth to make manifest those forces gained in its passage. In entering, the entity takes on those forms that may be known in the dimensions of that plane which it occupies, there being not only three dimensions as of the earth but there may be seven as in Mercury, or four in Venus, or five in Jupiter. There may be only one as in Mars. There may be many more as in those of Neptune, or they may become even as nil—until purified in Saturn's fires.

Reading 136–8

As the entity moves from sphere to sphere, it seeks its way to the home, to the face of the Creator, the Father, the first cause.

Reading 136–83

. . . self is lost in that of attaining for itself the nearer and nearer approach that builds in manifested form, whether in the Pleiades, Arcturus, Gemini, or in Earth, in Arcturus, Vulcan, or in Neptune. . . . as light, a ray that does not end, lives on and on, until it becomes one in essence with the source of light."

Editor's Note: One of the most fascinating concepts to come through Edgar Cayce's discourses were his teachings about soul activity in dimensions related to the other planets in this star system, *between* Earth incarnations, and how these affect our present lives. Here are some of these discourses.

The following is an example of a complete reading document.

Text of Reading 5755-1

This psychic reading given by Edgar Cayce at his office of the Association for Research and Enlightenment, Inc., Virginia Beach, Va., at the Seventh Annual Congress of the A.R.E., this 27th day of June, 1938, in pursuant to request made by those present.

PRESENT

Edgar Cayce; Gertrude Cayce, Conductor; Gladys Davis, Steno. Hugh Lynn Cayce, Gladys & Chas. Dillman from Youngstown, O., Maud M. Lewis from Greenville, Ala., Anna E. Hendley & Edna B. Harrell from D.C., Lillian McLaughlin,

Gladys & Thos. Jenkins, Reginia Dunn, Florence Evylinn
Campbell, Mary A. Miller, Alice M. Eddy, Irene Harrison,
Louise Chisholm, Henry Hardwicke, Jennie Moore and Leslie
Savage from N.Y., Mabel M. Applewhite from Newport News,
Va., Frances Y. Morrow, Edith & Florence Edmonds, Hannah
Miller, Ruth LeNoir, Helen Ellington, Margaret Wilkins, Esther
Wynne, Abbie Kemp & Malcolm H. Allen from Norfolk, Va. &
Helen Williams, Louise Tatum, Mara Edmonstone, Mrs. R.G.
Barr, Mrs. W.T. Sawyer, Grace & Geo. Ross from Virginia Beach.

READING

Time of Reading 3:35 to 4:20 P. M.

GC: In all Life Readings given through this channel there are references to sojourns of the soul–entity between incarnations on the earth
plane, in various planes of consciousness represented by the other planets in our solar system. You will give at this time a discourse which will
explain what takes place in soul development in each of these states of
consciousness in their order relative to the evolution of the soul; explaining what laws govern this movement from plane to plane, their
influence on life in this earth plane and what if any relationship these
planes have to astrology. Questions.

EC: Yes, we have the information and sources from which same may
be obtained as to individual experiences, sojourns and their influence.

As we find, in attempting to give a coherent explanation of that as
may be sought, or as may be made applicable in the experience of
individuals who seek to apply such information, it is well that an individual soul–entity, the record of whose astrological and earthly sojourns
you have, be used as an example.

Then a comparison may be drawn for those who would judge same
from the astrological aspects, as well as from the astrological or planetary sojourns of such individuals.

What better example may be used, then, than this entity with whom
you are dealing [EC? Case 294]

Rather than the aspects of the material sojourn, then, we would give
them from the astrological:

From an astrological aspect, then, the greater influence at the entrance of this entity that ye call Cayce was from Uranus. Here we find the extremes. The sojourn in Uranus was arrived at from what type of experience or activity of the entity? As Bainbridge, the entity in the material sojourn was a wastrel, one who considered only self; having to know the extremes in the own experience as well as others. Hence the entity was drawn to that environ. Or, how did the Master put it? "As the tree falls, so does it lie." [Eccl. 11:3 by Solomon. Where did Jesus say it?] Then in the Uranian sojourn there are the influences from the astrological aspects of *extremes*; and counted in thy own days from the very position of that attunement, that tone, that color. For it is not strange that music, color, vibration are all a part of the planets, just as the planets are a part—and a pattern—of the whole universe. Hence to that attunement which it had merited, which it had meted in itself, was the entity drawn for the experience. What form, what shape?

The birth of the entity into Uranus was not from the earth into Uranus, but from those stages of consciousness through which each entity or soul passes. It passes into oblivion as it were, save for its consciousness that there is a way, there is a light, there is an understanding, there have been failures and there are needs for help. Then help *consciously* is sought!

Hence the entity passes along those stages that some have seen as planes, some have seen as steps, some have seen as cycles, and some have experienced as places.

How far? How far is tomorrow to any soul? How far is yesterday from thy consciousness?

You are *in* same (that is, all time as one time), yet become gradually aware of it; passing through, then, as it were, God's record or book of consciousness or of remembrance; for meeting, being measured out as it were to that to which thou hast attained.

Who hath sought? Who hath understood?

Only they that seek shall find!

Then, born in what body? That as befits that plane of consciousness; the *extremes*, as ye would term same.

As to what body—what has thou abused? What hast thou used? What hast thou applied? What has thou neglected in thy extremes, thy extremities?

These are consciousnesses, these are bodies.

To give them form or shape—you have no word, you have no form in a three-dimensional world or plane of consciousness to give it to one in the seventh—have you?

Hence that's the form—we might say—"Have You?"

What is the form of this in thy consciousness? It rather indicates that everyone is questioned, "Have you?—Have You?"

That might be called the form. It is that which is thy concept of that being asked thyself—not that ye have formed of another.

With that sojourn then the entity finds need for, as it were, the giving expression of same again (the answering of "Have You?") in that sphere of consciousness in which there is a way in and through which one may become aware of the experience, the expression and the manifesting of same in a three-dimensional plane.

Hence the entity was born into the earth under what signs? Pisces, ye say. Yet astrologically from the records, these are some two signs off in thy reckoning.

Then from what is the influence drawn? Not merely because Pisces is accredited with an influence of such a nature, but because it is! And the "Have You" becomes then "There Is" or "I Am" in materiality or flesh, or material forces—even as He who has passed this way!

The entity as Bainbridge was born in the English land under the *sign*, as ye would term, of Scorpio; or from Venus as the second influence.

We find that the activity of the same entity in the earthly experience before that, in a French sojourn, followed the entrance into Venus.

What was the life there? How the application?

A child of love! A child of love—the most hopeful of all experiences of any that may come into a material existence; and to some in the earth that most dreaded, that most feared!

These side remarks become more overburdening than what you are trying to obtain! but you've opened a big subject, haven't you?)

In Venus the body-form is near to that in the three dimensional plane. For it is what may be said to be rather *all*-inclusive! For it is that ye would call love—which, to be sure, may be licentious, selfish; which also may be so large, so inclusive as to take on the less of self and more of the ideal, more of that which is *giving*.

What is love? Then what is Venus? It is beauty, love, hope, charity—yet all of these have their extremes. But these extremes are not in the expressive nature or manner as may be found in that tone or attunement of Uranus; for they (in Venus) are more in the order that they blend as one with another.

So the entity passed through that experience, and on entering into materiality abused same; as the wastrel who sought those expressions of same in the loveliness for self alone, without giving—giving of self in return for same.

Hence we find the influences wielded in the sojourn of the entity from the astrological aspects or emotions of the mental nature are the ruling, yet must be governed by a standard.

And when self is the standard, it becomes very distorted in materiality.

Before that we find the influence was drawn for a universality of activity from Jupiter; in those experiences of the entity's sojourn or activity as the minister or teacher in Lucius. For the entity gave for the gospel's sake, a love, an activity and a hope through things that had become as of a universal nature.

Yet coming into the Roman influence from the earthly sojourn in Troy, we find that the entity through the Jupiterian environment was trained—as we understand—by being tempered to give self from the very universality, the very bigness of those activities in Jupiter.

For the sojourn in Troy was as the soldier, the carrying out of the order given, with a claim for activities pertaining to world affairs—a spreading.

What form, ye ask, did he take? That which may be described as in the circle with the dot, in which there is the turning within ever if ye will know the answer to thy problems; no matter in what stage of thy consciousness ye may be. For "Lo, I meet thee *within* thy holy temple," is the promise.

And the pattern is ever, "have you?" In other words, have you love? or the circle within, and not for self? but that He that giveth power, that meeteth within, many be magnified?

Have you rather abased self that the glory may be magnified that thou didst have with Him before the worlds were, before a division of consciousness came?

These become as it were a part of thy experiences, then, through the astrological sojourns or environs from which all take their turn, their attunement.

And we find that the experience of the entity before that, as Uhjltd, was from even without the sphere of thine own orb; for the entity came from those centers about which thine own solar system moves—in Arcturus.

For there had come from those activities, in Uhjltd, the knowledge of the oneness, and of those forces and powers that would set as it were the universality of its relationships, through its unity of purpose in all spheres of human experience; by the entity becoming how? Not aliens, then—not bastards before the Lord—but sons—co-heirs with Him in the Father's kingdom.

Yet the quick return to the earthly sojourn in Troy, and the abuse of these, the turning of these for self—in the activities attempted—brought about the changes that were wrought.

But the entrance into the Ra Ta experience, when there was the journeying from materiality—or the being translated in materiality as Ra Ta—was from the infinity forces, or from the Sun; with those influences that draw upon the planet itself, the earth and all those about same.

Is it any wonder that in the ignorance of the earth the activities of that entity were turned into that influence called the sun worshippers? This was because of the abilities of its influences in the experiences of each individual, and the effect upon those things of the earth in nature itself; because of the atmosphere, the forces as they take form from the vapors created even by same; and the very natures or influences upon vegetation!

The very natures or influences from the elemental forces themselves were drawn in those activities of the elements within the earth, that could give off their vibrations because of the influences that attracted or draw away from one another.

This was produced by that which had come into the experiences in materiality, or into being, as the very nature of water with the sun's rays; or the ruler of thy own little solar system, thy own little nature in the form ye may see in the earth!

Hence we find how, as ye draw your patterns from these, that they become a part of the whole. For ye are *relatively* related to all that ye have contacted in materiality, mentality, spirituality! All of these are a portion of thyself in the material plane.

In taking form they become a mental body with its longings for its home, with right and righteousness.

Then that ye know as thy mental self is the form taken, with all of its variations as combined from the things it has been within, without, and in relationship to the activities in materiality as well as in the spheres or various consciousness of "Have you—love, the circle, the Son?"

These become then as the signs of the entity, and ye may draw these from the pattern which has been set. Just as the desert experience, the lines drawn in the temple as represented by the pyramid, the sun, the water, the well, the sea and the ships upon same—because of the very nature of expression—become the *pattern* of the entity in this material plane.

Draw ye then from that which has been shown ye by the paralleling of thy own experiences in the earth. For they each take their form, their symbol, their sound, their color, their stone. For they all bear a relationship one to another, according to what they have done about, "The Lord is in his holy temple, let all the earth keep silent!"

He that would know his own way, his own relationships to Creative Forces or God, may seek through the promises in Him; as set in Jesus of Nazareth—He passeth by! Will ye have Him enter and sup with thee?

Open then thy heart, thy consciousness, for *he* would tarry with thee! We are through.

Reading 1895-1

The experiences of the entity in the interims of planetary sojourns between the earthly manifestations become the innate mental urges, that may or may not at times be a part of the day dreaming, or the thought and meditation of the inmost self.

Hence we find astrological aspects and influence in the experience, but rather because of the entity's sojourn in the environ than because of a certain star, constellation or even zodiacal sign being in such and such a position at the time of birth.

Know that man—as has been expressed—was given dominion over

all, and in the understanding of same may use all of the laws as pertaining to same for his benefit.

In the application of same as a benefit—if it is for self-indulgence or self-expression alone, it loses its own individuality in the personality of that sought or desired; and thus the very knowledge may be used as a stumbling-stone. But if each experience is as a manifestation to the glory of a creative or heavenly force, or that which is continual thus the judgements being drawn from an ideal that is spiritual in its concept, then there is the greater growth, the greater harmony—for there becomes an at-onement with the influences about same.

Reading 281-55

Q: *Through other planetary sojourns an entity has the opportunity to change its rate of vibration so as to be attracted in the earth plane under another soul number.*

A: Each planetary influence vibrates at a different rate of vibration. An entity entering that influence enters that vibration; not necessary that he change, but it is the grace of God that he may! It is part of the universal consciousness, the universal law.

Reading 1947-1

In giving the urges, then, we find that the astrological influences are not so much because of the certain position of the Sun or the Moon or the Stars, but because of their relationship which is a relativity of influence or force; for, being from the body or materialization, there is the activity of the soul in the environs in which certain influences have been and are accredited to the activities from those planetary sojourns. Thus they become as signs, omens in the experience.

Reading 2599-1

In giving the interpretations of the records as we find them here, these are chosen with the desire and purpose that this be a helpful experience for the entity; enabling it to better fulfill that purpose for which it entered this experience.

Know that one's manifestations in the earth are not by chance but a fulfillment of those purposes the Creative Forces have with each individual entity.

For, the Creative Influence is mindful ever, and hath not willed that any soul should perish, but hath with every temptation prepared a way, a means of escape.

Thus the very fact of a material manifestation should become an awareness to the individual entity of the mindfulness of that influence of Creative Energy in the experience.

Then, as to the abilities with this entity—magnify the virtues, minimize the faults—not only in thy judgments of others. For with what judgment ye mete, it will be meted to thee again.

Thus the purpose of each experience is that the entity may magnify and glorify that which is good. For, good is of the one source, God, and is eternal.

Then as an individual entity magnifies that which is good, and minimizes that which is false, it grows in grace, in knowledge, in understanding.

Know that in the manner ye mete, or do to thy fellow man, so ye do unto thy Maker.

Then let it be from this premise that the judgments and the activities of this entity in this material experience may be drawn as a helpful force in its journey through this particular sojourn.

From the sources of the previous sojourns we find urges arising materially in the experience of the entity—that is, from the previous earthly sojourns as well as the astrological sojourns during the interims between earthly manifestations.

Not that there are influences from the position of stars, planets or the like that may not be met; but these are as urges—just as the environs of an individual in the material plane produce urges, because of studies or activities in a given direction, and because certain material abilities are innately a part of the entity's experience. Yet urges oft arise in the experience of an entity for this or that, the source of which the entity itself may not understand or comprehend—for no one in the family thought or acted in that direction.

Then, this—the environ of the entity, the soul manifesting in the earth—may be called by another name, as with this entity—a part of the present name in the experience before this; and the abilities as an individual to meet others, to influence them in the activities in which certain interests might be magnified, come from the entity's activities in the previous sojourn.

Thus the earthly sojourns make for manifested urges in the present experience. Also those planetary sojourns, in this present solar system, make for urges that are accredited to those particular planets as states of consciousness—that become innately manifested in the present entity.

For instance, in this entity we find the manifestation of Mercury, Venus, Jupiter, Uranus—manifested and latent in the dreams, the visions, the activities; in the high mental abilities of the entity, the ability to reason things through, the stableness of its activity in using not only material but mental forces as an influence to urge others to buy or to be interested in, or to analyze conditions.

Thus in the present, and manifestedly so, the entity might find the abilities as an adjuster, or as an individual to give expression as to evaluation of materials or properties, or abilities of individuals.

In Venus we find that appreciation of the beautiful, as related to art, as related to things, as related to conditions in the relationships of groups of peoples one to another.

Also from Jupiter we find the association with groups, masses, as a reflection in the activities of abilities, and that in which the entity may apply itself in the present experience.

Uranus brings the extremes, in which the entity may rise to great heights of expectation and yet at times find self in a wonderment. Yet innately there are those expectancies in spiritual facts, in the occult, in the psychic forces, that are powers of might for either good or evil. For, as indicated, in Uranus there are the extremes.

Know, as from the first premise, that no influence surpasses the *will* of an individual. The power of will is that birthright as the gift from the Creative Force to each entity, that it may become one with that Influence; knowing itself to be itself yet a part of and one with the Creative Influence as the directing influence in the experience.

Also the earthly sojourns bring urges through the latent faculties of the sensory forces; or they become characteristics that may be indicated—either latent or manifested—as the power or might manifesting; for only as the entity works with or against an influence does it become magnified in the experiences of the entity.

Reading 243-10

In entering, we find, astrologically, the entity coming under the influence of Mercury, Mars, Jupiter, Venus, and Neptune. These, as we find, have builded, and have influenced the entity, in the present experience. Also we find urges as respecting the experiences as related to innate urges, and that as has been *builded* in the present entity.

Aside: Let not this be confusing, as to innate urges and that as is builded in the present experience, for the application of will, and of innate urge through planetary influences, is exercised in this entity as we would find it in few.

In the experience, then, we find these as builded *irrespective* of will, and those that have been builded as respecting the *application* of will's influence; for *will* is that developing factor with which an entity chooses or builds that freedom, or that of being free, knowing the truth as is applicable in the experience, and in the various experiences as has been builded; for that builded must be met, whether in thought or in deed; for thoughts are deeds, and their current run is through the whole of the influence in an *entity's* experience. Hence, as was given, "He that hateth his brother has committed as great a sin as he that slayeth a man," for the deed is as of an accomplishment in the mental being, which is the builder for every entity.

Much has been met, much as been *builded* by the entity in the present experience. Much has been experienced by the entity in the various spheres through which the entity has passed.

In that builded, we find one of high, ennobling ideas and ideals; often tempered in Mars, through wrath, that has brought does bring, will bring, many of the experiences that have been experienced in the building of the entity's inner being to the action within the life.

In those influences in Jupiter, finds for the bigness of the entity's vision, the broadness of the good or bad that may be wielded in the influence of those whom the entity contacts from time to time, or period to period, or experience to experience.

In those influences seen in those of Neptune, brings for those of that as is of the *mystery* in the experiences of the entity; the associations in many peculiar circumstances and conditions; the conditions and experiences, and influences, as bring many conditions as, by others, would be misunderstood (and there *be* minds that would misunderstand, rather than know the truth).

In the experiences there has been *innately* built, the fear of evil in the life, the fear of those that would bring condemnation on those who are in power, and oft is the entity too *good* to others for its own good! Through the attempt innate to build that which would be the releasing of those experiences which have been had by the entity.

In those influences seen in Neptune, also brings that water—large *bodies* of water—the entity will gain most through the experience, has gained and will gain, through sojourn near, or passing over, large bodies of water, and *salt* water is preferable; for in the experiences will be seen, fresh hasn't *always* meant for living water.

In those as builded innately, we find:

One that is in that position of making friends easily, and just as easily losing same; yet there are friendships made that make for the better understanding in the experience, and in those of *Venus* forces comes the love that is *innate* in the experience of the entity. Through all the vicissitudes of life this remaineth, for the entity has gained much that makes for that as was given—"There is a friend that sticketh closer than a brother," and "he that is just kind to the least of these, my little ones, is greater than he that hath taken a mighty city." These building, these kept within the consciousness of the entity, will build to that Christ consciousness as makes all free; for in Him is the life, and He is the light that shineth into the dark places, even to the recesses of that of His own consciousness that makes for that which casteth out fear; (for being afraid is the first consciousness of sin's entering in, for he that is made afraid has lost consciousness of self's own heritage with the Son; for we are heirs through Him to that Kingdom that is beyond all that that would make afraid, or that would cause a doubt in the heart of any. Through the recesses of the heart, then, search out that that would make afraid, casting out fear, and *He* alone may guide.)

Editor's Note: The group working with Edgar Cayce attempted to develop tests that would help individuals identify their planetary influences

and their past-life influences. Cayce said that only the astrological was attainable, given that past lives required reading the Akashic Record of a soul or the soul awakening to its memories of past life. He guided them to use this astrological information for helping to identify one's vocation. Here's that reading:

Text of Reading 5753-3

This Psychic Reading given by Edgar Cayce at his home on Arctic Crescent, Virginia Beach, Va., this 25th day of October, 1939, in accordance with request made by Hugh Lynn Cayce, Manager of the Ass'n for Research & Enlightenment, Inc.

PRESENT

Edgar Cayce; Gertrude Cayce, Conductor; Gladys Davis, Steno. Hugh Lynn Cayce.

READING

Time of Reading 11:30 to 11:40 A. M. Eastern Standard Time.

GC: You will have before you the psychic work of Edgar Cayce relative to information from Life Readings concerning vocational guidance; together with the entity, the enquiring mind, Hugh Lynn Cayce, present here, who seeks to correlate and use such information. From a study of the Life Readings it would seem that an individual's mental and spiritual development, his contentment, is dependent upon releasing and expression of basic mental and emotional urges coming from planetary sojourns and past incarnations. Please give at this time suggestions for the development of a system or a series of intelligence tests which will reveal these basic urges and help an individual in selecting a life's work. It is hoped that such information as may be given here may be developed and used through scout activities and the Princess Anne Schools. You will answer questions.

EC: Yes, we have the information here, that has been indicated in Life Readings as to vocational guidance for individuals.

In developing a plan, or a manner of seeking ways in which individuals might give expression of the latent faculties and powers from the material sojourns, as well as the planetary influences—here we will find that there are conflicting forces and influences at times—as we have indicated.

The astrological aspects may give a tendency, an inclination; and a systematic, scientific study of same would indicate the vocation. And about eighty percent of the individuals would be in the position of being influenced by such astrological aspects; or would be in the position for their abilities to be indicated from same.

But the other twenty percent would not be in that position, due to the influences from activity or the use of their abilities in material experience. Hence in these it would be not only necessary that their material sojourns be given, but as to what had been accomplished through same, and that to be met in the present experience. For, as has been indicated, no influence—astrologically or from material sojourns—surpasses the will or the determination of the individual. Then, there are material factors that rule or govern or direct or influence such forces. These may be tempered by the astrological aspects, but these are not (the astrological aspects) the major influence or force—the will.

Thus, only about eighty percent of the individuals may have their abilities indicated from the astrological aspects in the direction of vocational guidance, as to be a determining factor for such.

If some five individuals would be taken, and their charts or astrological aspects indicated, and questions asked as to determining the influence or force from same—from such an aspect there might be given information so that a general chart might be indicated for a questionnaire, or a test, or an activity that would be of material benefit in a great *number* of individuals—but never a perfect score may be indicated. For the will, as well as the factors of environment, have their influence.

Ready for questions.

Q: How can the urges from past incarnations be determined by a test or series of tests?

A: As just indicated—this may only be done by giving the material sojourns of the individual.

But if the astrological aspects and influences are given, then there may be determined a questionnaire from same.

Q: Should the chart be drawn from the geocentric or the heliocentric system?

A: The geocentric system would be the more in keeping with the Persian force or influence.

Q: Any other suggestion to Hugh Lynn Cayce regarding the development of this at this time?

A: As indicated, there may be charts drawn of five individuals, and a questionnaire may be determined for factors in the individual experience—as to what their inclinations or activities are. Not by telling, but by questioning!

Then *from* same, as indicated, there may be given a more correct or direct questionnaire that would be helpful for a large *number* of individuals—but *not* a perfect score.

For in about twenty percent of the populace at the present time, it is dependent upon what the individuals have done with their urges *through* material sojourns.

As indicated trough this channel, some are in keeping with the astrological charts, others are found to be partially so, others are diametrically opposed to same—because of the activities of the individuals.

We are through for the present.

Editor's Note: Cayce's discourses state that all souls were created at the same moment, yet Cayce used the term "old soul" occasionally. He later explained that he meant a soul that has been sojourning in and around Earth for many lifetimes. The following is a reading for an old soul, and this reading has many interesting references to planetary and constellational sojourning.

Text of Reading 436-2 M 28
(Elevator Boy, Christian with East Indian leaning)

This psychic reading given by Edgar Cayce at Lillian Edgerton, Inc., 267 Fifth Ave., N.Y.C., this 10th day of November, 1933, in accordance with request made by self—Mr. [436], Active Member of the Ass'n for Research & Enlightenment, Inc.

PRESENT

Edgar Cayce; Hugh Lynn Cayce, Conductor; Gladys Davis, Steno. Mr. [436].

READING

Born March 29, 1905, (11:30 P.M.) in Midland, Virginia.

Time of Reading 3:00 to 3:50 P. M. Eastern Standard Time . . . , D.C.

(Life Reading Suggestion)

EC: Yes, we have the entity and those relations with the universe and universal forces, that are latent and exhibited in the personalities of the present entity, [436].

It would be well to comment upon the oldness of this soul, especially in its activities—as will be seen—in periods when the occult and mystic influences were manifested in the experience of the entity in the earth; and make for influences that have been (or may be made) very good or very bad in the experience of the entity. Hence, this is an old soul.

In giving the personalities and the individuality of the entity in the present experience, we must approach same from the astrological, though these in the very fact of that given respecting its activities in the earth during such periods when such changes or activities were manifested in the material affairs of individuals, make for little that may be compulsory in astrological influence. Yet *impulses* arise from these influences.

As in passing from Pisces into Aries, there are those influences innately and manifested in the mental forces of the body; much of both of these, and they become conflicting in the experience at times of the entity.

Pisces brings rather the mystery and creative forces, and magnanimous aspects in students of—or in the thought of—influences in the active principles of individual impulse; with Aries bringing reason, or air, or airy actions, yet reason, more than Pisces would make the demands in the self at time for reasons for every manifestation, whether material conditions, mental or spiritual conditions in the experience of the entity. And at other periods it may be said that the entity becomes rather susceptible to influences about the body, without considering seriously the sources of the information and as to whether same is able to be verified by others or not. Feelings of same impress the entity from this astrological influence, which—as we see—does not only control earth's sojourn but the position of the entity in this sojourn through the planetary influences in the earth's solar system.

As to the sojourns in the astrological influences then, we find these are the ruling; not from their position at the birth, but rather from the position of the entity's activities in that environ.

Mars is an influence rather from the associations then, in self's own experience. Or when dissensions, distrust, dissatisfaction, madness, wars, arise; these come *about* the entity rather than influencing the *activities* of the entity, other than through the associations with individuals that make demands upon the entity and its activities in these directions. These become at times concrete experiences in the entity's activities in the present experience; yet these, as we find, for many a year now (and these began some three years ago) will be less in the experience until Mars in '38 or '39 becomes nearer in its influence upon the sojourners of those in the earth that have experienced a sojourn in that environ.

Hence this may be said, in a manner, to be of little influence then in the period, or during that period, when the entity should make for a stabilization in self's experience of that to which it may develop its better abilities in this present sojourn in the earth.

From Venus rather a complex position or condition comes to the experience of the entity, where filial or marital or such relations as of loves in the material earth come in the experience. Not that there hasn't been, nor won't be, nor isn't existent, that which is pure, elevating and helpful in the experience of the entity in its relationships with individuals of both sexes in this way and manner; yet these have brought some very pleasant experiences and some very contrary and contradictory influences in the activities and in the experience of the entity in the present.

Hence it may be given in passing, to the entity, that the love of and for a pure body is the most sacred experience in an entity's earth sojourn; yet these conditions soured, these conditions turned into vitrol, may become the torments of an exemplary body, and one well-meaning, and make for loss of purposes.

Keep the friendships, then. Keep those relationships that are founded upon all that is constructive in earth, in the mind, in the spirit.

As to those influences from the sojourn of the entity in Uranian forces, as may be indicated from that given as to the oldness and as to the delving into the occult and mystic and the application in the experience, the entity has sojourned more than once in this environ and under quite varied or different experiences and manifestations. Hence there are periods when earthly conditions, mental conditions, spiritual conditions, are very good; and others when all are very bad in the experience of the entity in the present. Yet, as we find, in the application of self as related to the impulses that may rise in the consciousness of the entity in the present experience from those impulses received from the sojourns, these may be made the strong fort in the activities of self in the present. But they must be tempered, from the very experiences in the sojourn, to making for not an active force in those experiences from planetary influences in a weak body, but turn to strengthening the body-physical for the manifestations of the correct raising of those vital energies in the material body, through which such influences may make for manifestations and experiences in the earth's sojourn. These influences from Uranus make for many of the ills that have been in the experience in the body, in the nervous reactions to the physical body, to the weak experiences to the physical body, when the very vital life force of a material body was in danger of being separated from physical for an ethereal sojourn.

As to the appearances, then, and their influence in the present, these are given as the ones influencing the activities of the present body; rather than numbers, we give those that make for the greater activity in the present:

Before this we find the entity was in the land of nativity, and about those places, those peoples, where the first settlings were—and the first sojournings that spread beyond the mere force builded; or about that town that was the first capitol of this new land, or this portion of same. And among the activities there are many of those things being reconstructed, re-enacted, that will be not only of physical interest but will, with the application of the abilities within self, recall to the entity many of the associations that the entity had with the peoples of the land (native). While the entity did not go what is proverbially called "native" in the experience, the associations were such, with those that acted in the capacity of the spiritual leaders (or with what were termed the medicine men of the period), and with those that later attempted to set themselves as leaders of this people, that the entity made friends both with the natives and the colonists, aiding the colonists in the period to establish better relations; in the name then Edward Compton, a distant family name even that may be found among those that sojourned in the peninsula land of that portion of the country.

The entity lost and gained through the experience; gained in the application of self for the benefiting of those with whom the entity sojourned, and the natives also whom the entity aided in making better cooperative relationships in the activities of the people of the period and time. The entity aided in establishing such relationships that there was the trading of the native peoples in distant lands. One particular period of interest, that may be noted in history, was when the entity aided in bringing to the peoples corn from the western portion of their native land, that sustained those peoples through a very bad period.

From that period there is the influence oft in the present in those activities when studies of those peoples are the experience of the entity, and there are both confusing and constructive influences. Yet, when about many of a mediumistic turn, many of those with whom the entity engaged in life and activity would attempt to speak to the entity; especially one that termed himself Big Rock, Black Rock.

Before this we find the entity was during that period when there were the returnings of those peoples in the land now called Greece, from the rebellions that had been active in Mesopotamia and in the regions about what is known as Turkey and those lands; during those periods of Xenophon's activities and those wars.

The entity was among the few of these natives, strong in body, purposeful in intent, to return to the native land; and the entity gained through the experience but lost in the latter portion of the sojourn when returning to the native land, when power was entrusted in the activities of the entity; and while the purposefulness was correct, there arose those that distrusted and brought contentions by the accusations brought against the entity, in the name Xerxion. Then Xerxion lost in faith in his fellow man, and the faith in the purposefulness of those that were attributing to the gods, or the powers and forces as they were named and termed, the elements to maintain the equilibrium. Hence in that the entity lost, and in the present—while there are those abilities in self to lead for a purposefulness in its activity, too oft has the entity become discouraged when accusations of unkind things were brought, or when experiences made for the losing of confidences in friends and associates it has made discouragements too easily in the experience in the present. This (in passing, may be said) is a test period for the entity in its relationship, particularly. Hence the entity should turn to the abilities within and find self first, knowing in what, in whom the entity has believed; knowing He is able to keep that which is committed unto Him against any experience that may arise in the lives or activities of those who are His loved ones, His chosen. Who has He chosen? They that do His biddings. What are His biddings? Love the Lord thy God with all thine heart (and thy God meaning Him that in Spirit is the Creative Forces of all that is manifested), keeping self unspotted from the world or any smirch of activity, and loving thy neighbor, thy brother, as thine self. These will make for the relieving of all those influences in the experience, and bring harmony, peace, joy, understanding, in the experience of the entity; and will enable the entity to not only study, not only to understand, but—best of all—to comprehend from what source many of those influences arise, as we will see has to do upon the mental body of the entity, and become active oft in the physical forces or the physical activities through their nerve reflexes in a material body.

Before this we find the entity was in that land now known as the Egyptian, during that period when there was the returning of those that had been astrayed through the sending away of the priest of the land.

The entity was among those that were banished with the priest, being with the priest Ra Ta in the association and in the activities of gathering together the tenets that the scribe—in a way; rather the one gathering the data than one scribing or protecting the data—collected. The entity aided the priest specifically in some of the associations and connections with those of the temple gatherers to whom the priest gave heart and mind; and for the act among those the entity was severely punished when banished by the natives, rather than the king. Yet, being healed by the priest in the foreign land, the entity came again into Egypt when there was the re-establishing, and aided in rebuilding the temples of service; being active then in what today would be called the preparations for those things that kept the cleansings of the temple after use of individual in body, or as a caretaker (termed in the present) of offices, temples, churches or buildings. Then the entity was in the name Pth–Lerr. The entity gained and gained, and much that is suffered in body is as a bringing to bear of that which may make the mental contact with the tenets of the experience.

One might ask (this aside, please), why would such be brought to bear? Because, with the experience of the entity in the period, seeing the developments and the activities, there was set within the soul that desire: "Come what may, whatever is necessary in my whole experience of my soul, make me to know again the joys of the tenets of Ra Ta."

In the present these may mean much, if they are builded for a soul development in the present; for these needs be to overcome those experiences in the sojourn just previous in the Atlantean land.

Before this we find the entity in the Atlantean land rather rebelled with those forces of Baalilal, with those activities in the electrical appliances, when these were used by those peoples to make for beautiful buildings without but temples of sin within.

The entity, in the name Saail, was a priest (demoted) in the Temple of Oz in Atlantis, and lost from soul development, gained from material things; yet these fade, these make raids upon the body in physical manifestations. These make for hindrances in activity in that known within the innate self. For, rather were the mysteries of the black arts as applied in the experience practiced by Saail, yet these in the present may be turned into account in material things in making material connections; but use or apply same in the experience rather in the mental and spiritual manner for the soul development of the entity, rather than for materiality in the present. These are weaknesses, then, yet weakness is only strength misapplied or used in vain ways.

Before this we find the entity was in that land that has been termed Zu, or Lemuria, or Mu. This was before the sojourn of peoples in perfect body form; rather when they may be said to have been able to—through those developments of the period—be in the body or out of the body and act upon materiality. In the spirit or in flesh these made those things, those influences, that brought destruction; for the atmospheric pressure in the earth in the period was quite different from that experienced by the physical being of today.

The entity then was in the name Mmuum, or rather those calls that make easy the mysteries of words as related to sounds and rote that bring to the consciousness, in those that have indwelled in those lands, that activity that merits (not the word), that brings, that impulse that urges that those forces from without act upon the elements in whatever sphere they may bring a material manifestation. This must be controlled within self, from those influences in [436]; for these are those things at times that hinder.

Let self, then, be grounded rather in the faith of that which is, was, and ever will be, the source of all spirit, all thought all mind, all physical manifestation—the *one* God, as called in this period. In that period he was called Zu-u-u-u-u; in the next Ohm—Oh-u-m; in the next (now known as Egypt) with Ra Ta, He was called God—G-o-r-r-d!

As to the abilities of the entity, and that to which it may attain, and how, in the present:

First it may be said, study—through that known in self of the spiritual and mental forces active in the experience of the body—to show self approved unto an ideal that is set in the Son, the Christ, knowing that in possessing the consciousness of His love, His manifestation, all is well; for, as is known, without that love as He manifested among men, nothing can, nothing did, nothing will come into consciousness of matter. Not that we may deny evil and banish it, but supplanting and rooting out evil in the experience, replacing same with the love that is in the consciousness of the body Jesus, the Christ, we may do all things in His name; and using those opportunities in whatsoever sphere of activity the entity may find to show forth those commands He gave, "If ye love me, keep my commandments." What, ye ask, are His commandments? "A new commandment give I unto you, that ye love one another." What, then, are the fruits of love? The fruits of the spirit; which are kindness, hope, fellowship, brotherly love, friendship, patience; these are the fruits of the spirit; these are the commands of Him that ye manifest them in whatsoever place ye find yourself, and your soul shall grow in grace, in knowledge, in understanding, and that joy that comes with a perfect knowledge in Him brings the joys of earth, the joys of the mental mind, or joys of the spheres, and the *glory* of the Father in thine experience.

Ready for questions.

Q: *When will adverse planetary change for better influences in my life?*

A: As indicated, the receding of Mars brings, and has brought, better planetary influences; as the mental activities and applications in the light of the love in Christ brings with those activities in the coming closer and closer of Venus with Uranus; which begins in December, present year, for the approach, reaching nearer conjunction in May or June of the coming year better conditions, mentally, materially, financially.

Q: *What is the main purpose of this incarnation?*

A: To set self aright as respecting the variations in those tenets in the first two experiences in the sojourn, tempered in those tenets given in Ra Ta—that, "The Lord Thy God is *one!*" And manifesting of that oneness in the little things makes the soul grow in His grace!

We are through for the present.

Editor's Note: Cayce even gave readings on how to subdue negative influences from planetary or astrological soul activity. Here's one example:

Text of Reading 137-18 M 27
(Stockbroker, Hebrew)

This psychic reading given by Edgar Cayce at his office, 322 Grafton Avenue, Dayton, Ohio, this 24th day of July, 1925, in accordance with request made by self—Mr. [137].

PRESENT

Edgar Cayce; Mrs. Cayce, Conductor; Gladys Davis, Steno.

READING

Born October 28, 1898, in New York City. On the floor of Time of Reading the New York Stock 9:30 A. M. Dayton Savings Time. Exchange, Wall & New Streets, N.Y.

GC: You will have before you the body of [137], on the floor of the N.Y. Stock Exchange, Wall & New Streets, New York City, N.Y., with the information as has been given this body in readings given for same on the 28th day of October, 1924, also that given on the 12th day of January, 1925, [See 137-4 and 137-12] especially that portion of same relating to the undue influences in the life of [137] when Moon's forces square to

Saturn and Mars bring doubts within the body's mental forces. This is given in reading of January 12th, as occurring in the week of August 13, 1925. You will please tell us just the character of influence that will occur, whether of mental, spiritual or physical forces, and how this entity may guard against this influence.

EC: Yes, we have the body here, and the information as has been given this body in regards to influences as are exercised in the life of the entity at the periods given, through position of the planetary forces as are exercised in the life of same.

Now, we find that with the indwelling urges as are seen within the individual, when there occur certain positions of those planetary influences under which the body (meaning spiritual force body) has developed, these bring the intense urge towards those experiences of the entity as it passed through that phase of its development, for we find the urge within each entity is its experiences in all phases of its existence, plus the environmental conditions of body at time, with the will of entity counterbalancing same through body–mind urge. Hence the necessity of each entity understanding, having knowledge of those laws that do govern same in the material or physical realm, as well as those pertaining to the spiritual forces as are manifest through the body in each of its various changes, for we find all are one, for the real body is that spiritual force manifesting in same, always through the Trinity of that comprising same.

In the information as has been given as we find, these influences come for this body at this particular or special time, when through the influences as are exercised in the position Moon, Jupiter, with Saturn and with Mars, this brings to that body, [137], those of that urge, that doubt of self and self's abilities to manifest either mental (Moon with Saturn), with physical, (doubting of own physical health, see?) through the forces or powers in Mars, the own spiritual forces as is the influence, or undue influence on Jupiter's forces with this position as manifested. Then, we find these at this time pertaining to this nature:

The body–mind, the spiritual–mind, has reached at this period, especially, and during week of August 13, 1925, that place where the doubts of every nature, pertaining to this threefold force as is given here, come to the body. Hence, we will find, will be easily aggravated through any mental association, whether in business relation, moral relations socially or marital relations, for, seemingly, at this time would occur all of these combining with one to bring the detrimental forces to the mind. With the condition of mind comes that condition where the physical forces, apparently, respond more to these of the conditions wherein weaknesses are shown or manifested in same. Then the combination of all would bring as to that—well—"I don't care! What difference does it make? Let it go to pot!"—See?

Then, to overcome this, rather place those forces as are manifest through will forces, knowing that these do appear. That, "Get thee behind me Saturn (Satan), that I *will* serve the living God, with *my* body, *my* mind, *my* money, *my* spirit, *my* soul, for I am *His*, and through *me*, my body, my mind, do I manifest *my* impression, *my* interpretation of *my* God."

This does, not, as we see, relate to physical accidents, physical conditions, physical things, pertaining to the material things of life, save as would be affected by same through—"Well, I don't care."

We are through for the present.

9

●

Communicating with the Spirit Realm

Editor's Note: From Cayce's perspective, communicating with people who were not incarnate (spirits/ghosts) was simply another aspect of the psychic sense. However, he was not a supporter of Ouija boards and seances, preferring communications that he considered more healthy—ones that did not lead to confusion about and distraction from a soul's incarnate purposes and relationships. Yet, as the following discourses will show, he taught that these spirit communications have a place in the full spectrum of life and the psychic sense.

Text of Reading 5756-4

This Psychic Reading given by Edgar Cayce at his office, 115 West 35th Street, Virginia Beach, Virginia, this 17th day of March, 1927, in accordance with request made by Edgar Cayce himself and [900].

PRESENT

Edgar Cayce; Gertrude Cayce, Conductor; Gladys Davis, Steno.

READING

Time of Reading 11:40 to 12:40 P. M. New York, N.Y.

GC: You will have before you all the information that has been given in psychic readings by Edgar Cayce concerning communication with those who have passed into the spirit plane. You will correlate all of this information in a systematic way and manner, that this may be understood by the conscious mind of any individual studying the subject, and you will answer all questions that I will ask you concerning this subject that should be answered. You will continue with such information which was begun yesterday, March 16, 1927, in 5756-3.

EC: (After having the first suggestion repeated and being told to continue) Yes.

Now, we have the information here, and that as has been given.
[Continuing:]

First, let it be understood there is the pattern in the material or physical plane of every condition as exists in the cosmic or spiritual plane, for things spiritual and things material are but those same conditions raised to a different condition of the same element—for all force is as of one force.

In that period when the spirit, or when the soul, (best that these be classified, that these be not misunderstood, then, in their relations one to another) is in the material, the body physically composed of the physical body, the mind, and the soul, add the subconscious mind, and the superconscious mind, or the spirit.

In the make-up of the active forces of the physical body, it (the body) is constituted of many, many, cells—each with its individual world within itself, controlled by the spirit that is everlasting, and guided by that of the soul, which is a counterpart—or the breath that makes that body individual, and when the body is changed, and this is the soul body, the elements as are patterned are of the same.

That is, that builded by thought and deed becomes the active particles, atoms, that make up that soul body, see?

When the soul passes, then, from the physical body, it (the soul body) then constituted with those atoms of thought (that are mind) and are of the Creative Forces a part, and then we have the soul body, with the mind, the subconscious mind, its attributes—which have been explained or given heretofore, as the relation of what the subconscious mind is— which never forgets, and is then as the sensuous [conscious] mind of the soul body; the spirit or superconscious mind being that as the subconscious mind of the material body—the place, then, of the resident or residence, or that occupied by the soul body becomes to the finite mind the first question. The occupancy is at once—as is seen here, there are about us many, *many*, many, soul bodies; those upon whom the thought of an individual, the whole being of an individual is attracted to, by that element of thought—just the same as the action in the material body—for remember, we are patterned, see? one as of another. In the next, then, we find that, that as *builded* by that soul is as the residence of that soul, the companion with that as has been builded by that soul—either of the earthbound or of that element or sphere, or plane, that has its attraction through that created in that soul being in the actions, by the thoughts, of that as an individual. Hence we find there are presented the same conditions in the astral or cosmic world, or cosmic consciousness, as is present in the material plane—until the consciousness of that soul has reached that development wherein such a soul is raised to that consciousness *above* the earth's sphere, or earth's attractive forces—until it reaches up, up, outward, until included in the *all*, see?

In the next step, then, we find, as regarding information given, the ability of such a body, or entity, to communicate with those in the material plane:

Question and answers are often confusing, by those that give or supply information concerning such experiences; for each experience is as individual as the individual that receives same, or the entity that transmits same, and the possibility, probability, the *ability*, of individuals to so communicate, or so draw on those forces, is raised, limited, or gained, by the act of the individual seeking its ability to so communicate—for, remembering, conditions are not changed. We find individuals at times communicative. At other times uncommunicative. There are moods, and there are moods. There are conditions in which such conditions are easily attained. There are others that are hard, as it were, to meet or cope with. The same condition remains in that distant sphere—as is felt by many—when it is the *same* sphere, *unless* the individual, or the entity, has passed on.

Then the next question that arises is: How are such communications brought about? Just as given. When the body (material) attunes self to that plane wherein the sensuous consciousness is in obeisance to the laws of physical or material, and the spiritual or astral laws are effective, those of the astral plane may communicate, in thought, in power, in form. What form, then, do such bodies assume? The desired form as is built and made by that individual in its experience through the material plane. Remembering our pattern. We find bodies are made by the action of cell units in the material body. Some to beauty, some to distress by that merited for the physical experience. Hence a necessity of a physical experience, that the *desires* that build may be made, changed, or acted upon.

Again we return to the astral or the soul body. In the various forms of communication, why, *why*, is such communication so often of seemingly an unnecessary nature, or seemingly inadequate to the mind of the soul entity, as understood by the mind of one hearing, seeing, or experiencing, such a communication? As may be illustrated in: The message as may be received from the boy just passed into the spirit world, and able through mediumistic forces of someone to communicate to mother, "All is well. Do not grieve. Do not long for the change." Such seems to be in the nature of rebuke to a sensuous mind when momentous questions as might be propounded, could be, or would be—as some mind would say—given. Remember the pattern as is set before. Is the greeting, *is* the greeting of some profound questions the first meeting? Rather cultivate that of such communications, and receive the answer to that of the most profound that may be propounded in any way and manner to those seeking such information. Is such information always true? Always true, so far as the individual has brought self into that attunement as is necessary for the perfect understanding of same. Do not attempt to govern information, or judge information, by the incorrect law, see? When force is taken, what is the impelling force such as is seen in the movement of material objects? When under stress, the communication or the appearance of the soul body is in contact with the individual mind; such as we have seen and experienced through that of the information as has been given. Such impelling forces, we find, are the combination of that in the individual receiving and in the abilities of the individual so communicating—that is, we find that in the various experiences of individuals, levitation, or objects that are of material nature, are moved about by the active principle of the *individual through whom such manifestations are being made*, and not by spirit action, or soul action. Yet *controlled* by that cosmic consciousness. Don't leave that out, see? Controlled—for, as given, the body must be subjugated that such force may manifest. Then we see undue strength, undue power, is seen exercised at such periods. True—for things that are controlled by spirit alone are of a great deal greater active force than of the sensuous mind, as a trained mind is more active than one untrained.

Now many questions have been given. Many various forms of the active forces of communicative energies, or of soul forces, as are manifested in the spirit world and in the material world, have been given—but these as we have given here are set forth that those who would study may have the basis of an understanding that will give each and everyone that knowledge that the physical world, and the cosmic world, or the astral world, are one—for the consciousness, the sensuous-consciousness, is as the growth from the subconsciousness into the material world. The growth in the astral world is the growth, or the digesting and the building of that same oneness in the spirit, the conscious, the subconscious, the cosmic, or the astral world. We find, from one to another, individuals—individuals—retained in that oneness, until each is made one in the Great Whole—the Creative Energy of the Universal Forces as are ever manifest in the material plane.

We are ready for the questions that may be asked, as we see here, concerning various conditions—for many are gathered about to give their various experiences as have been passed through in this transition period.

Q: *Is it possible for those that have passed into the spirit plane to at all times communicate with those in the earth plane?*

A: Yes and no—for these conditions are as has been described—that the *necessary* way or mode must be prepared; for as this: Ever has that vibration as is attracted and thrown off been active in the world as is exercised through that called the telephone, but without proper connection, without shorts, without any disturbance, may proper communication be made! These have not always been active to the *physical* body. These are not always in proper accord to be used by the physical body. Just the same in that pattern. Those in the astral plane are not always ready. Those in the physical plane are not always ready. What conditions arise (is asked) that we in the physical plane are not ready? The *mind*! What conditions arise that we in the astral plane are not ready? There are those same elements as has been outlined, of that of the development going on, and the willingness of that *individual* to communicate, as given, see? but when set aright, these may—until passed into that Oneness, or returned again, or gone on beyond such communications.

Q: What physical thing may an individual do to be able to communicate with those that have passed into the spirit plane?

A: Lay aside the carnal or sensuous mind and desire that those who would use that mentality, that soul, for its vehicle of expression, do so in the manner chosen by that soul; for some communicate in act, in sight, in movement, in voice, in writing, in drawing, in speaking, and in the various forces as are manifest—for force is *one* force.

Q: What form or body does the spirit entity assume upon leaving the earth or material body?

A: Just as given. That builded by the body in its experience. We illustrate: Would one of a uniform body desire a change—would one of a crippled body desire a change the answer, as has oft been given: *act* that way, *it*—the result, the change—comes about.

Q: Where is the dwelling place of such spirit entities?

A: That that such entity has builded, and as it (the entity) draws about it, or desires same shall be. In the earth's plane many are attracted by those conditions and are held by many loved ones, when their desires to be on the way, as it were. Building in that way and manner as is in its heart of hearts, soul of soul, to be about. See? Now, the dwelling place is as builded by that entity, and in that place about the earth and the earth's sphere, time is no time, space no space, to such entities.

Q: Is the effort for spirit communication as much effort on the part of the spirit entity as the effort that should be made on the part of the material or physical entity?

A: The force should never be applied, and may never be applied and be real, in either case. The willingness and the desire from both is necessary for the perfect communication, see? Illustrate this same condition by that physical condition as is seen in attunement of either that called radio, or of that called phone, or that of any of that vibratory force as is set by the electron in the material plane. Necessary for the perfect union that each be in accord. In other words, we find many in the astral plane *seeking* to give force active in the material. Many in the material *seeking* to delve into the astral. They must be made one, would they bring the better.

Q: *What form of consciousness does the spirit entity assume?*

A: That of the subconscious consciousness, as known in the material plane, or the acts and deeds, and thoughts, done in the body, are ever present before that being. Then consider what a hell digged by some, and what a haven and heaven builded by many.

Q: *What are the powers of the spirit entity?*

A: Raised to the highest power as is developed in that plane, and are—as outlined—as *varying* as individual's power or ability to manifest, or to exercise that manifestation, in the material. We have not changed, see? for as we would say: What is the power of an individual in the *physical* plane? Naught as it enters. Naught until it reaches that ability to *give* of self in service. Yet, as we find, there is in all the world nothing that offers so much possibility as when the body of the human is born into the material plane. In the minds of every other, nothing offers more beautiful condition, raised to its same power, as the birth into that of the astral plane. Hence, how oft, how oft, is such seen in this entering! How expectant becomes both? Does it become a wonder at that vision as Stephen sees, when "My Lord, standing ready to *receive* me," see?

Q: *Is it possible for those passing into the spiritual plane to be conscious of both the material and the spiritual plane?*

A: Just as given. Just as is seen in the various experiences of those who are spiritually minded—yet many carnal minds have passed from the body for days before they realized they were passed. Sensuousness!

Q: *Describe to me what (Mrs. [3776]) saw as she entered the spirit plane, when she said "Mrs. [139] says she will guide me over."*

A: Just that same experience as has just been described. The desire in the mind—soul mind—and the physical mind, to be at a oneness, one with the other, and to give to each that as necessary for that wonderful development possible in that plane—for, as is seen, we find as this experience in *this* condition: The mind in that accord with the soul forces, in action, meets those who are the active in that of the aid in the development. Hence we find this very active force in the soul body, Mrs. [139] ready—and with that consciousness of the conditions in action going on—guiding and meeting the soul body in its transition, and the spirit body, mind, soul, attuned in that of the physical body, (Mrs. [3776]), so it answers one with another, and is capable of being hearkened back or to such condition, see?

Q: How may force act in unmaterialized form—i.e. without matter to embrace in itself the many individual self consciousness separated by space in the material form—i.e. man, but all one inner self in the cosmic or 4th dimension?

A: Just in the manner as has been described and given, in how that the transition of one force becomes as the portion of the whole force. As is, that each is the pattern, one of another, or as may be illustrated: How does the force or power transmitted from the powerhouse light each individual globe in the city? Each have their connection. Each have their various forms, or their various powers, according to that as has been set. Now, applying same in the illustrative forces, we find each being in accord, each being in the direct connection, each apply, manifest, according to that as is builded in the individual in its transition, or in its experience, and as the various forces are manifested each give off that as is taken on.

We are through for the present.

Reading 900-330

Q: In regard to the educational work in my connection with the Association, I am now entering upon that phase of the phenomena called Spirit Communication. I have experienced this myself quite frequently of late, in a very natural and pronounced manner. Will you give any special kind of reading that I may ask for in relation to these particular and personal experiences?

A: As has been given as respecting spirit communication, these are of the individual nature, and are of rather the individual interpretation, and when such are presented through, of, for, or on any other way or manner, there may be the suspect of there entering in other force than that of individual importance of individual understanding.

In the matter of spirit communication:

As is seen, as has been given, there are ever about those in the flesh in the earth's plane those desiring to communicate with those in the earth plane, attracted by the act, intent and purport of the individual, or by the act, intent, purport, of that entity in the spirit plane.

In these as have been, as are being presented to this body, [900], these are above the ordinary experiences, and are of the definite position, condition, and represent definite phases in the understanding of the entity.

Study same, then, with that same knowledge as was given of old, that God the Father speaks to Himself through man and man's activities in the earth. The spirit is of the Father, and all force is of God. Study these from this phase. As to information concerning definite or specific instances of communication, these may receive—through these sources— the interpretation, either of the giver, or of those associated in the spirit plane with such entities, see? for various phases of such communication present themselves much as the various phases of the development of entities, and those intents, those purports as were once set forth by Saul of Tarsus, are as near the correct interpretation of spirit communication as may be attained in any literature or writings that may be attained at the present period.

Prepare that thou art preparing concerning such conditions, and these will equal—or even be better understood than that as was given by him in those passages concerning the gifts of the spirit. Read same.

Q: What part of the Bible?

A: Paul—in the Epistle to the Corinthians.

Reading 900-363

That of the correct understanding will give the better understanding of spirit communication, or the activity of the forces from cosmic plane activity in the material forces; remembering, then, first there must be proper attunement for the correct understanding of *any* condition presented to a sensuous mind. From the present then, we find that given of "Seek and ye shall find," in its broaden sense is answered in that experienced here. That is, when self desires—and puts desire in action, with self in attunement in the spiritual sense—that same reasoning as spoken of self's subconscious self gives answer from within, and accorded to by cosmic forces in attunement with that desired. Hence the feeling of innate action separated from cosmic forces, or urge, or push. This then gives one the understanding that though there may be many urges from without and within, unless self has lost through inactivity the power of self, then self's action accorded by will is ever the stronger force, whether related to those urges from the physical surroundings and all its elements of urge, or from spiritual surroundings with its urge from developed or from cosmic entities' action on same; for self remains ever the portion of the whole, irrespective of those elements that have to do with either the mental materialness or the spiritual activity actualities of that plane. Hence like begets like, and man—or the *being* itself—is the pilot, director and keeper of self.

Prayers for the Dead—

Reading 281-15

Q: Please give a prayer for those who have passed on?

A: Father, in Thy love, Thy mercy, be Thou near those who are in—and have recently entered—the borderland. May I aid, when Thou seest that Thou canst use me.

Reading 2280-1

Q: Can you tell me if my older son, who passed away last May, died of natural causes or was he killed?

A: An accident.

Q: Can I be of any help to my sons now? If so, how?

A: Prayer for those who are seeking a way, *the* way to the light, aids ever.

As ye meditate—as ye pray—for as thy body is indeed the temple of the living God, there He hath promised to meet thee—then as ye meet Him, thy Maker, thy Lord—pray that there may be the light, the help needed, that they may be guided in that way and manner which will bring all together in the way as *he*, thy Lord, would have it.

Q: Can you tell me how they are developing, and what is happening to them?

A: This ye may find the better within thyself. For as ye seek, as ye speak with Life—the Lord—*there* ye may know as to what, as to how they each are developing.

Reading 281–4

Q: Will the forces please give us information regarding [5546, male child mentally retarded] passing on? Did we aid him? If so, how?

A: Here we find a physical condition of a nature that was of prenatal conditions, where a physical being was in existence with only half an awareness of the conditions about same. The *releasing* of that force into the ability to become aware, or a birth into the spiritual sources. Not only aiding the individual but those so responsible for same, as to bring a consciousness of the universal or creative spiritual forces in the lives—lives of all. Aid, then, not only to the body but to those so vitally interested in the same.

Reading 281–19

Q: Were we able to help C.H.H. before he passed on? And why did I feel so confident that he would recover? May some enlightenment be given?

A: As each seeks to give expression of that felt within self, it may be of the *best* of seed; yet seed falls upon all characters of soil, even as He has shown. Yet those that would sow the word of truth, or that would manifest His love as the sower, *falter* not. Aid came. Be not discouraged. It will bear fruit.

Reading 2276–4

Q: To what extent was [5678's husband] helped by our prayers, mentally, physically or spiritually?

A: Still gaining from same!

Q: Can we help him further?

A: If he is still gaining, you can still help him!

. . . there should not be wholly discouragements; and not necessarily a resignedness, but rather the attitude of being a channel, being used in the way and manner as the divine influence within would have thee be.

Let thy prayer be:

"In Thy hands, O God, I commit my estate, my being. Thou knowest that which is needed for that manner of expression in which I may make that union with Thee in the Christ. May all things be done in order and in keeping with Thy will."

10

●

Our Destiny Beyond Death

Reading 900-147

Q: Is this a revelation—a revelation of that I was pondering—what is meant by Life Eternal?

A: Life Eternal—One with that Oneness, as is seen by the Soul becoming One with the Will, the spirit, of the Father, even as is shown in the ensample of the Man called Jesus—the Christ, the Savior of the World, through compliance to those same laws, as He complied with, see? for with that Force, that Spirit, brought in the World, then becomes the truth, "What thou asketh in My name, believing in thine heart, same shall be unto thee." *Beautiful* is the life and the feet of those who walk in the paths of the righteous One. Lo! The Heavens open and I see Him stand at that Way which leads unto Life Everlasting; *that* then the Way, the Truth, the Light, the Water of Life, the Man made Perfect in that Spirit of Him who gave Himself as the ransom for many.

In this is the ransom then: Making self of low estate, as is called in man's realm. All powerful—yet never using that power, save to help, to assist, to give aid, to give succor to someone who is not in that position to help or aid self, see?

Reading 262-75

First, then, to define destiny—that is in accord with truth: Destiny is

129

of the next three lessons that would be given through here. Then, destiny is of what? *Mind, body, soul*. The next three lessons: Mind, body, soul.

Destiny is, then, a law—an immutable law, that is as lasting as that which brought all into being that is manifested in all the varied spheres of materialization, or manifestation; and that of which man has seen the signs here, there, written in those experiences of the travelers along the varied spheres of experience. Man in the interpretation of those signs has often mistaken the sign for the law.

Hence to those that hold to this or that theory, then, this group would present—in reference to the destiny of mind, of body, of soul—that which may become as a light to many who have stumbled upon those signs in their activities, in their efforts here and there.

Then, in giving that from which and upon which ye as individuals have applied and may apply as a group in giving an aid to others, in making their paths straight, look ye to the *law* that is destiny—destined—in the Word of Him. For He gave that though the heavens and the earth pass away, His Word shall *not* pass away. What is the gospel? What *is* the truth? What is the judgment? What is the law?

"As a man thinketh in his heart, so is he"? ye ask. "As ye do it unto the least of these, my little ones, ye do it unto me"? another asks. "As ye would that men should do unto you, do ye even so to them" says another.

What gave He as the last command? "A new commandment I give unto you, Love one another." What is thy lesson on Love? How many live same in their daily experience?

But ye ask again, What of destiny? He hath not willed that any soul should perish but that *every* soul shall know the will of God to *do* it!

Then, ye wonder—can such be possible in threescore and ten years in the earth? Also ye wonder—doth the time of birth, the place of the environment, make or have a part in destiny? Do the days or the years, or the numbers, all have their part? Yea, more than that! Yet, as has been given, all these are but signs along the way; they are but omens; they are but the marks that have indicated—for, as given, He has set His mark, and these are *signs*, not the destinies! For the destiny of the mind, of the body, of the soul, is with Him. For naught that man may do maketh for the righteousness, but the mercy of the Father as exemplified in the Son makes for the destinies of that trinity of the mind, the body, the soul, in its effort, in its endeavor, in any environ, in any experience, to mark the way; yea, even so clearly that there may not be longer the stumbling, the wandering—for the day of the Lord draweth nigh for many. While ye wander, search thine own heart and *know* as of old that faith is counted as righteousness to those that love the Lord. Those of ye study that ye show yourselves approved unto Him that giveth life; that would direct the mind, that manifests in the body, that would have thy soul as a *companion* with Him—thy elder brother! Who hath *opened* the gates of heaven, who hath closed—to you that manifest love—the gates of hell! For He hath given. And he that confesseth that Jesus is the Christ, the Son of the living God, hath *life* eternal—and the gates of hell shall *not* prevail against him!

What, then, is thy Destiny? It is made in that thou pervertest not that thou *knowest* to do in thine heart respecting thy fellow man! For ye look to Him who is the author and the finisher of faith. He *is* Faith, *and* Truth, *and* Light—and in no other is there comeliness at all. For He is the rock of salvation; the bright, the morning star; the rose of Sharon; the *wonderful* counsellor. In Him *is* thy Destiny. Turn ye not away from Him.

As to those things that are marks, signs, omens along the way—*understand* them for what they *are*! Put *not* thy trust in *them*! For He has given (and remember He gave, "Heavens and the earth may pass, but my Word shall not!"); he that seeks shall find; he that knocketh, to *him* shall be opened. For He hath spoken, and His word is; that "Though ye wander far afield, though ye become beset by the doubts and the fears, though ye even turn thy back upon *me*, if ye will remember the promises and *turn*, I *will hear*—*speedily*—and will forgive thy trespasses, even as *you* forgive those that trespass against you."

Let love be without dissimulation. Look not upon that which may bring only joy to thee, yet even peace to thee; for He is thy light and thy guide. Put rather thy life, thy *experiences*, thy associations, even thine own self, into His keeping; knowing He is able to keep that thou hast committed unto Him—and may save thee, for He alone hath the words of life. And no matter what ye make or mark, or mar, He is *still* with thee, ready to harken when ye call.

Let thine heart be raised, then, in praise that thou hast *named* the

Name above every other name; for He alone can save—and He alone can *forgive*—He alone can answer prayer; to the same measure that *thou*, *in* thine own experience, *answereth* the prayer of thy fellow man.

Reading 262–77

That individuals may of their own volition choose the exaltation of self, or the aggrandizement of self's own ego, is apparent. This makes for what many have termed and do term their karmic conditions, that may then be seen.

Those who are in that way or attitude of "Let the words of my mouth and the meditation of the heart be acceptable in Thy sight," are in the way of truth.

Those that kick against the pricks—even as thine own teacher, thine own writer, Paul, saw the error and turned therein. Was it destiny that he was to be called? Or that the gift of the Son set a way, a vine, a water, living water, and that he chose to meditate and thus give that destined to work upon? For, as given, this material life is of those energies that make for the adherence to the laws that pertain to this material plane. And the spiritual laws are interpenetrable with those activities that make for the will of the Father that no soul should perish but that there may be the burning of the dross that it may be sifted as wheat, that it may be purified even as He through suffering in the material things that *are* for the soul's edification.

Then, in this may each be enabled to look only to Him, knowing that He *is* the light, He *is* the way; those things which come to bear in the experience are that there may be known those things necessary for those who seek, for only those who seek may find.

For, as has been given, there be nothing in earth, in hell, in heaven, that may separate the soul from God save the individual soul.

Then, what is destiny? That the soul who seeks shall the sooner find; that the soul who puts into practice day by day that which is known may the sooner enjoin itself to that which *is* hope and peace and happiness and love and joy in the earth.

That there should be those who should know heaven on earth or in the earth, or in flesh, is the destiny of those that are willing, who have had their minds, their bodies, their souls cleansed in the blood of the

Lamb. How? By being as He, a living example of that He, the Christ, professed to be.

Then, that which hinders most—this group, any group, the world—is speaking one thing and living in the inner self another. This destines to bring confusion and turmoil and strife and want, and a reckoning with that which makes for tears, sorrow, and that is of the earth earthy. And ye are, as He gave, servants of—workers with—*that* force whom ye serve.

In presenting self, then, as has been given, come to the altar of truth within thine own self. There He through His promise, *in* His promise, will meet thee, and it shall be shown thee that which is the way, the manner.

Individuals in their understanding falter here and there, for they have been told and have listened from their own observation, rather than experience, that this way, that way, the prayer at this period or at that period, the stars at this period have meant or do indicate or do mean that this number from the name, this day means this or that, and in the application comes confusion. These—as has been given—are signs, are omens; but how gavest He? "The heavens and the earth will pass away, but my word shall not pass away."

The signs, the omens then, are to be used as stepping-stones for an *understanding*; not to be confused with nor given—through that gift in thee of constructive forces from the Father-God Himself—other power than they contain within themselves. For each soul that meets and encounters and accredits receives the same in return. How gave He on this? "He that receiveth a prophet in the name of a prophet hath a prophet's reward." This does not indicate that the prophet received is of God, an angel of heaven or of hell; but in the name, in the manner, in the way as received so cometh the reward *that* is destined! Why? In the seed of thought, whether of body, mind or soul, *is* the seed thereof; and it bears fruit which is of its own kind and nature. Said He, "Ye do not gather grapes from thistles; neither may ye expect to do evil looking for good." For the destiny is in that which has set the world, yea, the earth and all that is therein, in motion. And ye in thy blindness, thy foolishness, thy *desire* for self, look for some *easy* way; when all the ease, all the hope, all the life there is *is* in Him! Then, *His* way is the easy way. What is His way? "He that would force thee to go one mile, go with him twain;

he that would sue thee and take away thy coat, give him thy cloak also." Did He say whether justly or unjustly? Who did He say is the judge? "Judge not that ye be not judged." For, "As ye do it unto the least in the earth, ye do it unto me."

Then, when ye seek to do His biddings and do otherwise than thou would have Him do unto thee, thou alone maketh the way harder for thyself. For the will of the Father is *life*! It is life eternal to as many as will accept, as many as will view that which they hear from the still small voice as they meet Him within. For ye are made up of mind, body, soul. The soul is the God-part in thee, the *living* God. The manifestations that ye make in thy mind make for that growth which is manifested in the body in the earth and in thy soul in the everlasting.

So, know ye the way; point it out. For, as He has given, though ye come to the altar or to thine church or to thine group or to thine neighbor pleading not for self but for others, and it is that ye may be exalted, that ye may be honored, that ye may be spoken well of, for others; He cannot hear thy petition. Why? Because there has another entered with thee into thy chamber, thy closet, and He thy God—that answers prayer, that forgives through His Son—is shut out. In His name, then, only; for, as He gave, "They that climb up some other way are thieves and robbers."

Then, today, will ye not rededicate thyself, thy body, thy soul, to the service of thy God? And He that came has promised, "When ye ask in my name, *that* will be given thee in the earth." Then, do not become impatient that ye are counted in this day as a servant, as an humble worker, as one that is troubled as to food, shelter, or those things that would make thy temporal surroundings the better. For ye grow weary in waiting, but the Lord will not tarry; eternity is *long*, and in that ye may spend it in those things that are joy and peace and harmony, make thy self sure in Him. How? "As ye do it unto these, my brethren, ye do it unto me." Just being kind! Thy destiny is in *Him*. Are ye taking Him with thee in love into thy associations with thy fellow man, or art thou seeking thy *own* glorification, exaltation, or thine own fame, or that ye may even be well-spoken of? When ye do, ye shut Him away.

Enter thou into thy chamber not made with hands, but eternal; for there He has promised to meet thee. There alone may ye meet Him and be guided to those things that will make this life, now, happiness, joy and understanding.

As ye have received, love ye one another even as He has loved you, who gave up heaven and all its power, all its glory, that thine mind can conceive, and came into the earth in flesh that ye through Him might have the access to the Father, God. In Him there is no variableness or shadow made by turning. Then, neither must thy thoughts or thy acts cause a frown or a shadow upon thy brother—even as He. For He gave, "Be ye perfect, even as thy heavenly Father is perfect." Ye say, "This cannot be done in this house of clay!" Did He? Ye say, "This is too hard for me!" Did he grumble, did He falter? To be sure, He cried, "Father, if it be possible, let this cup pass." Yea, oft will ye cry aloud, even as He. Ye cannot bear the burden alone, but He has promised and He is faithful, "If ye put thy yoke upon me, I will guide you."

Then, when we come in our sorrows alone and there comes the peace, the quiet, and then those periods of joy and gladnes when we forget— we carry the thought of others, of those that would make merry, and wonder why the joy has passed. It is because we have left Him outside.

Take Him, then, in thy joys, in thy sorrows, in all of thyself; for He alone hath the words of life.

Reading 412–9

Q: Along what lines should entity study to prepare for entity's destiny in the cosmic plane?

A: Study to show thyself approved unto that thou hast set as thy ideal in the spiritual plane; rightly divining the words of truth. For truth is life, life is light; and He is life, He is light, He is the Creative Force in thine experience. And keep self unspotted from condemnation of the world.

Q: Give guidance how to bring this idea into material manifestation.

A: Work at same as ye would the seam upon a garment. Ye do not stitch the whole seam at a flash, but one stitch at a time. Hence as has been given, it is precept upon precept, here a little, there a little; making practical application.

If ye would be happy (it is the law), ye must make others happy. Ye cannot know happiness unless ye experience that ye have brought happiness, hope, joy, into the experience of another.

This does not mean, then, becoming long–faced, melancholy; but rather *joyous, glad, hopeful*! But neither does it mean folding thy hands in indolence; rather as has been given, the harvest is white, the laborers are few. If ye would know Him, be up and doing. For as it was said, "He went about *doing* good." Not *being* good but *doing* good—which is the being good; being good for something, mentally, spiritually.

Mind is the Builder. Then, if ye would have less strife and more harmony, build same in thy daily relationships. For when ye complain of the faults of others, do ye not build such barriers that you cannot speak kindly or gently to those whom ye have felt or do feel have defrauded or would defraud thee? How spoke the Master?

"It is indeed necessary that offenses come, but woe unto him by whom they come." But "If thine enemy smite thee, turn the other cheek." *Living that, being that,* is to know the life eternal; and only in the manifesting of same, and bringing into materiality such experiences, may ye indeed *know* the joy even of living.

For how gave He? "Ye would not have *known*—had I not come." And His promises are sure! For though the heavens—yea, and the earth—pass, His words will not pass away.

Then in Him ye *can*, ye *may*, believe.

The A.R.E. Press publishes books, videos, and audiotapes meant to improve the quality of our readers' lives—personally, professionally, and spiritually. We hope our products support your endeavors to realize your career potential, to enhance your relationships, to improve your health, and to encourage you to make the changes necessary to live a loving, joyful, and fulfilling life.

For more information or to receive a free catalog, call:

800-333-4499

Or write:

A.R.E. Press
215 67th Street
Virginia Beach, VA 23451-2061

EDGAR CAYCE'S A.R.E.

What Is A.R.E.?

The Association for Research and Enlightenment, Inc., (A.R.E.©) was founded in 1931 to research and make available information on psychic development, dreams, holistic health, meditation, and life after death. As an open–membership research organization, the A.R.E. continues to study and publish such information, to initiate research, and to promote conferences, distance learning, and regional events. Edgar Cayce, the most documented psychic of our time, was the moving force in the establishment of A.R.E.

Who Was Edgar Cayce?

Edgar Cayce (1877–1945) was born on a farm near Hopkinsville, Ky. He was an average individual in most respects. Yet, throughout his life, he manifested one of the most remarkable psychic talents of all time. As a young man, he found that he was able to enter into a self–induced trance state, which enabled him to place his mind in contact with an unlimited source of information. While asleep, he could answer questions or give accurate discourses on any topic. These discourses, more than 14,000 in number, were transcribed as he spoke and are called "readings."

Given the name and location of an individual anywhere in the world, he could correctly describe a person's condition and outline a regiment of treatment. The consistent accuracy of his diagnoses and the effectiveness of the treatments he prescribed made him a medical phenomenon, and he came to be called the "father of holistic medicine."

Eventually, the scope of Cayce's readings expanded to include such subjects as world religions, philosophy, psychology, parapsychology, dreams, history, the missing years of Jesus, ancient civilizations, soul growth, psychic development, prophecy, and reincarnation.

A.R.E. Membership

People from all walks of life have discovered meaningful and life–transforming insights through membership in A.R.E. To learn more about Edgar Cayce's A.R.E. and how membership in the A.R.E. can enhance your life, visit our web site at EdgarCayce.org, or call us toll–free at 800-333-4499.

Edgar Cayce's A.R.E.
215 67th Street
Virginia Beach, VA 23451–2061

EDGARCAYCE.ORG